·大学生读书计划·

University Reader

英汉对照·中国文学宝库·古代文学系列

English-Chinese · Gems of Chinese Literature · *Classical*

唐诗选

Selected Poems from the Tang Dynasty

偬 仕 编

Compiled by Zong Shi

中国文学出版社

Chinese Literature Press

外语教学与研究出版社

Foreign Language Teaching and Research Press

图书在版编目(CIP)数据

唐诗选:英汉对照/偬仕编. —北京:中国文学出版社:外语教学与研究出版社,1999.8
(中国文学宝库·古代文学系列)
ISBN 7-5071-0530-X

Ⅰ.唐… Ⅱ.偬… Ⅲ.唐诗-中国-唐代-对照读物-英、汉 Ⅳ.H319.4:I

中国版本图书馆 CIP 数据核字(1999)第 23454 号

中文责编:吴善祥　沈洁莹
英文责编:殷　雯

英汉对照　中国文学宝库·古代文学系列
唐诗选
偬　仕 编

中国文学出版社
(北京百万庄路24号)
外语教学与研究出版社
(北京西三环北路19号)
出版发行

北京市鑫鑫印刷厂印刷
新华书店总店北京发行所经销

开本 850×1168　1/32　7.875 印张
1999 年 8 月第 1 版　1999 年 8 月第 1 次印刷
字数:142 千　印数:1—5000 册

ISBN 7-5071-0530-X/I·496
定价:10.90 元

目　录
CONTENTS

大学生读书计划

——中国文学宝库出版呼吁

在即将开机印刷这第一批50本名为中国文学宝库的英汉对照读本时，我们的心情竟然忧多于喜。因为我们只能以保守的5000册印数，去面对全国400万在校大学生。

虽然我们并非市场经济的局外者，若仅为印数（销售量）计，大可奋起而去生产诸如TOFEL应试指南，或者英语四六级模拟试题集一类的教辅图书，但我们还是决定宁可冒着债台高筑的风险，也有责任对大学生同胞发出一声亲切的呼唤：请亲近我们的中国文学。

身为向世界译介中国文学和向国内出版外语读物的，具有双重责任的出版社，我们得知目前大学生往往仅注重外语的学习而偏废了母语的提高，以及忽视了中国文学的阅读，放弃了人文知识的训练。有统计表明，某理工院校57%的同学不曾读过《红楼梦》等四大名著，以致校园内外流行着“样子像研究生，说话像大学生，作文像中学生，写字像小学生”的幽默。还有一副这样的对联，说大学生的文章是“无错不成文，病句错句破残句，句句不堪入目；有误方为篇，别字错字自造字，字字触目惊心”，横批“斯文扫地”。作为未来社会中坚和整个社会发展关键力量的大学生，这种“文弃”现象的流行，势必导致一场人文精神危机的爆发。对照以科学与人文精神追求为主题的五四新文化运动，八十年的历程告诉我们，以上提醒绝非危言耸听。

我们已经迈入知识经济时代，在追求科学知识的同时，创新精神已成为关键；而创新的源泉其实有赖于多学科多领域知识的交融，依靠的是新型的复合型人才，所以，文学对于新一代的大学生来说绝非装点，而是沟通自然科学与人文科学的桥梁，使我们在汲取知识的同时更能获得智慧，于创造物质的同时还进一步丰富和完善着精神；无怪乎爱因斯坦认为自己受影响最大的竟是陀思妥耶夫斯基。由此证明，一个真正的科学家应该拥有丰富的文学和文化知识以及完整的人格。十年前，七十五位诺贝尔奖得主聚会巴黎，当时他们所发表的宣言开篇就是，“如果人类要在21世纪生存下去，必须回首2500年去吸收孔子的智慧。”确实，十年的时间让我们有目共睹，现代经济科技的飞速发展何尝不是一柄双刃的剑？只有文化的力量才能抵消随之而来的负面后果。可见，知识的获取与技能的训练对于大学生来说固然重要，但文化与修养却尤需关切。正因为大学生代表着社会先知先觉的知识力量，置身当前的文化现实，就应有一分责任感与使命感，力求对知识技能以外许多带有根本性质的精神追求形成明确的意识，从而具备一种对生命意义进行探索与追问的精神，一种以人文精神为背景的生存勇气和人格力量。那么，能够引导我们探索前行的一盏明灯，不就是闪烁着理想光芒的不朽的文学名著吗？

一个人乃至一个民族，从其对文学的亲疏态度，可以衡量出其文化素质的程度。文学应是从人类文化中升华出的理想的结晶，她“使人的心灵变得高尚，使人的勇气、荣誉感、希望、尊严、同情心、怜悯心和牺牲精神复活起来”（威廉·福克纳）；无疑，只有文学才能从更高的层次上提升人的文化素质和整体素质，充实人的内心世界，焕发人的精神风貌，带给人们真善美。而亲近文学，特别是热爱祖国灿烂的文学以及文化，正是当代中国大学生加强文化修养，弘扬人文精神的有力脚步。

“越是民族的，就越是世界的”，中国文学属于中国，也属于世界。和平是人类的共同愿望，交流与共享则是新世纪的潮流。

中国当代大学生的血液里流动着数千年的文化积淀，没有理由在让世界了解中国大学生聪明才智的同时，却无缘分享我们的骄傲——中国大学生不但能够读懂英语的莎士比亚，而且能让世界感动于中国文学的伟大。

这是我们作为出版者的理想。我们原有一个世纪礼物的构想，是同大学生一起做一个"读书计划"。这一次将中国文学的最新荟萃配设高水平的英语译文，是其中推荐给新世纪大学生的第一批读物。盼望着您——我们无数知音中的5000名先来者，给我们鼓励，也给我们意见和批评。

编者

一九九九年五月三十日

只有文学才能从更高的层次上提升人的文化素质和整体素质，充实人的内心世界，焕发人的精神风貌，带给人们真善美。而亲近文学，特别是热爱祖国灿烂的文学以及文化，正是当代中国大学生加强文化修养，弘扬人文精神的有力脚步。

A Poem About a Cicada Written in Prison

Luo Binwang

Outside a cicada is stridulating in the depths of autumn,
Wile in jail I am tortured by a surge of homesickness.
Hoary-haired with grief, how can I endure
Such plaintive singing of the black-headed creature?
Heavy dew has encumbered it from taking wing,
Its sounds easily muffled by strong winds.
Nobody in the world trusts my noble and unsullied nature,
Who is there to vindicate my innocence?

在狱咏蝉

骆宾王

西陆蝉声唱，
南冠客思侵①。
那堪玄鬓影，
来对白头吟②。
露重飞难进，
风多响易沉③。
无人信高洁，
谁为表余心④？

① 西陆：指秋天。南冠：楚国的帽子，这里是囚犯的代称。客思：流落他乡而产生的思乡之情。侵：扰。

② 玄鬓：指蝉。古代妇女将鬓发梳为蝉翼之状，称为蝉鬓，这里以蝉鬓称蝉。白头吟：乐府曲名。一说“白头”指诗人自己，“吟”指蝉鸣。

③ “露重”两句是说，秋露浓重，寒蝉明翅也难以飞进，秋风飒飒，蝉的鸣叫声被风声淹没。

④ 高洁：古人认为蝉栖息在高树上，餐风饮露，清高纯洁。

英汉对照
English-Chinese
中国文学宝库
Gems of Chinese Literature
古代文学系列
Classical Literature

Pavilion of Prince Teng

Wang Bo

The Pavilion of Prince Teng towers high by the riverside,
But gone is the music amid tinkling jade pendants and carriage bells.
Painted pillars loom through the morning cloud from South Bay,
Pearly window curtains flutter in the evening rain from West Hills.
Only lazy clouds and shadows in the water are seen these long days,
Great changes have taken place in the years gone by.
Where is the prince who had the pavilion built here?
Beyond the balustrade silently the long river flows.

滕王阁

王　勃

滕王高阁临江渚，
珮玉鸣鸾罢歌舞[1]。
画栋朝飞南浦云，
珠帘暮卷西山雨[2]。
闲云潭影日悠悠，
物换星移几度秋。
阁中帝子今何在？
槛外长江空自流[3]。

---

① 渚：水边。鸾：刻有鸾鸟形的铃铛。这两句是说，赣江边上高耸的滕王阁，本是滕王欣赏歌舞的场所，滕王去后，歌舞也就停止了。

② 南浦：地名，在今江西省南昌市西南。西山：在今江西省南昌市西北，又名南昌山。

③ 帝子：皇帝的儿子，指滕王。槛：栏杆。长江：指赣江。

Bidding Deputy Magistrate Du Farewell

Wang Bo

The capital and palace are guarded by the land of three Qin kingdoms, [1]
In the distance the Five Ferries[2] are screened by wind and mist.
Now comes the time for us to bid farewell to each other,
And we will both be officials away from home on duty.
So long as we remain bosom friends in our heart of hearts,
We'll still feel like neighbours despite the distance apart.
So don't let us shed silly tears like youngsters,
At that last moment when we both wave goodbye.

---

① In the central part of present-day Shaanxi Province.
② Alluding to Sichuan Province because of the five big ferries along the Mingjiang River in the west of the region.

送杜少府之任蜀州

王　勃

城阙辅三秦，
风烟望五津①。
与君离别意，
同是宦游人②。
海内存知已，
天涯若比邻③。
无为在岐路，
儿女共沾巾④。

① 阙(què 确)：皇宫门前两边的楼观(guàn 贯)，也称望楼。城阙：指京城长安。辅：护卫。三秦：今陕西省关中地区，古为秦国，秦亡后，项羽分其地为雍、塞、翟三个王国，故称“三秦”。五津：长江自湔堰至犍为有白华津、万里津、江首津、涉头津、江南津等五渡口，合称“五津”。

② 君：指杜少府。宦游人：远离家乡出外作官的人。

③ 海内：四海之内，指国内。存：恤问，问候。

④ 无为：不要。岐路：岔路，指离别之处。

In the Mountains

Wang Bo

Long and miserably have I wandered along the Yangtze River,
Eagerly looking forward to returning to my home faraway.
All now is autumnal gloom in chilly wind,
While falling yellow leaves float all over the hills.

山 中

王 勃

长江悲已滞，
万里念将归；
况复高风晚，
山山黄叶飞。

英汉对照
English-Chinese
中国文学宝库
Gems of Chinese Literature
古代文学系列
Classical Literature

Following the Army to the Frontier

Yang Jiong

Flaring beacons relayed the alarm to the West Capital,
The scholar was filled with an ardent fighting spirit.
Holding the tally of command the general bade adieu to the palace,
And soon the iron cavalry besieged the Dragon City of Huns.
Army flags faded and dulled in the whirling snow,
While howling winds were punctuated by battle drums.
Better to join the army and be a captain
Than remain a scholar wallowing in books.

从军行

杨　炯

烽火照西京，
心中自不平①。
牙璋辞凤阙，
铁骑绕龙城②。
雪暗凋旗画，
风多杂鼓声③。
宁为百夫长，
胜作一书生④。

① 烽火：古代边境发生战争时，用以报警的信号。西京：长安。

② 牙璋：古代发兵所用的兵符，有两块，一留朝廷，一给主帅，两相嵌合，作为凭证。嵌合处为牙状，故称牙璋。这里代指将帅奉命出征。凤阙：汉长安建章宫东有凤阙，这里泛指皇宫。铁骑：强悍的骑兵。龙城：汉时匈奴大会祭天之处，故址在今蒙古人民共和国塔米尔河岸。

③ 凋：凋落，黯淡不明的样子。

④ 百夫长：卒长，泛指下级军官。

My Retreat by the Zhongnan Mountains

Wang Wei

Midway through life I set my heart on Truth
And have come to end my days by the Southern Hills;
When the mood takes me I stroll out alone,
My pleasure shared by none.
I walk to where streams rise,
Sit watching as the clouds drift up the sky,
And meeting with an old man in the woods
Talk and laugh with him, forgetting to return.

终南别业[①]

王　维

中岁颇好道，
晚家南山陲[②]。
兴来每独往，
胜事空自知[③]。
行到水穷处，
坐看云起时。
偶然值林叟，
谈笑无还期[④]。

① 终南别业：指长安附近终南山上作者的别墅。

② 中岁：中年。道：在这里指佛教的道理。南山陲：终南山上。

③ 胜事：快意的事。

④ 值：相遇。

英汉对照
English-Chinese
中国文学宝库
Gems of Chinese Literature
古代文学系列
Classical Literature

Wei River Farm

Wang Wei

A village in the setting sun;
Down humble lanes the cows and sheep wind home;
An old man, waiting for a shepherd boy,
Leans on his staff beside his wicker gate.
Pheasants are crying, wheat is in the ear;
Silkworms are dormant, sparse the mulberry leaves;
Up come two farmers shouldering their hoes
And meeting fall to talking...
Till, envying their carefree life,
I chant the sad old song *Longing for Home*.

渭川田家[1]

王　维

斜光照墟落[2]，
穷巷牛羊归。
野老念牧童，
倚杖候荆扉。
雉雊麦苗秀，
蚕眠桑叶稀[3]。
田夫荷锄立，
相见语依依。
即此羡闲逸，
怅然吟式微[4]。

① 渭川：即渭水，在陕西省。
② 斜光：斜阳。墟落：村落。
③ 雉(zhì)雊(gòu)：野鸡叫。蚕眠：蚕蜕皮时，不吃不动，叫眠。
④ 式微：这里用来表示作者欲归隐田园的意思。

英汉对照
English-Chinese
中国文学宝库
Gems of Chinese Literature
古代文学系列
Classical Literature

A Farewell

Wang Wei

I dismount from my horse and drink your wine.
I ask where you're going.
You say you are a failure.
And want to hibernate at the foot of Deep South Mountain.
Once you're gone no one will ask about you.
There are endless white clouds on the mountain.

送 别

王 维

下马饮君酒①，
问君何所之②？
君言不得意，
归卧南山陲。
但去莫复问③，
白云无尽时。

英汉对照
English-Chinese
中国文学宝库
Gems of Chinese Literature
古代文学系列
Classical Literature

① 饮(yǐn)君酒：谓请君饮酒。
② 何所之：到那里去。
③ "但去……"二句：你只管去，其他什么都不要问了。去欣赏大自然的美景，就足以自乐了。

Song About Xi Shi

Wang Wei

Her beauty casts a spell on everyone,
How could Xi Shi stay poor for long?
In the morning she was washing clothes in the Yue River;
In the evening she was a concubine in the Palace of Wu.
When she was poor, was she out of the ordinary?
Now rich, she is rare.
Her attendants apply her powders and rouge;
Others dress her in silks.
The king favors her and it fans her arrogance.
She can do no wrong.
Of her old friends who washed silks with her
None share her carriage.
In her village her best friend is ugly. It's hopeless
To imitate Lady Xi Shi's cunning frowns.

西施咏[1]

王　维

艳色天下重，
西施宁久微[2]？
朝为越溪女，
暮作吴宫妃。
贱日岂殊众？
贵来方悟稀。
邀人傅脂粉，
不自着罗衣[3]。
君宠益骄态，
君怜无是非。
当时浣纱伴，
莫得同车归。
持谢邻家子，
效颦安可希[4]！

---

① 西施：春秋时越国的美女。

② 宁久微：即岂会长久微贱的意思。

③ 邀人句：谓请人为她抹胭脂、扑香粉。傅，同“附”。

④ 持谢二句：相传西施邻居东施很丑，见西施心疼时颦(pín 皱眉)的样子很美，于是也学着捧心而颦，哪知这样一来，反而显得更难看了。持谢，用这件事告诉。邻家子，泛指旁人。安可，岂可。希，希求。

英汉对照
English-Chinese
中国文学宝库
Gems of Chinese Literature
古代文学系列
Classical Literature

An Autumn Evening in the Hills

Wang Wei

Through empty hills new washed by rain
As dusk descends the autumn comes;
Bright moonlight falls through pines,
Clear springs flow over stones;
The bamboos rustle as girls return from washing,
Lotus flowers stir as a fishing boat casts off;
Faded the fragrance of spring,
Yet, friend, there is enough to keep you here.

山居秋暝①

王　维

空山新雨后，
天气晚来秋。
明月松间照，
清泉石上流。
竹喧归浣女，
莲动下渔舟。
随意春芳歇，
王孙自可留②！

① 暝(míng)：晚。
② 随意二句：随意，自然而然地、照例地、自由地。王孙，贵人的子孙。春天的芳草虽然照例凋谢，秋景还是很美，王孙自可留居山中，不必归去。

Watching the Hunt

Wang Wei

A gusty wind, twang of horn-backed bows:
The general is hunting at Weicheng;
Hawks' eyes are keen above the withered grass,
Horse-hooves fall lightly where the snow has melted;
They wheel past Xinfeng Market,
And head home to the camp at Xiliu,
Turning once to mark where the vulture fell:
The plain sweeps far off to the evening clouds.

观　猎

王　维

风劲角弓鸣，
将军猎渭城①。
草枯鹰眼疾，
雪尽马蹄轻②。
忽过新丰市，
还归细柳营③。
回看射雕处，
千里暮云平④。

① 角弓：用角装饰成的弓。渭城：秦都咸阳。
② 鹰：猎鹰。
③ 新丰市：今陕西新丰。细柳营：汉代名将周亚夫驻兵的地方。
④ 雕：一名鹫，悍猛健飞。

英汉对照
English-Chinese
中国文学宝库
Gems of Chinese Literature
古代文学系列
Classical Literature

The Gully of Twittering Birds

Wang Wei

Idly I watch the cassia petals fall;
Silent the night and empty the spring hills;
The rising moon startles the mountain birds;
Which twitter fitfully in the spring gully.

鸟鸣涧

王 维

人闲桂花落，
夜静春山空。
月出惊山鸟，
时鸣春涧中。

英汉对照
English-Chinese
中国文学宝库
Gems of Chinese Literature
古代文学系列
Classical Literature

The Deer Enclosure

Wang Wei

Empty the hills, no man in sight,
Yet voices echo here;
Deep in the woods slanting sunlight,
Falls on the jade-green moss.

鹿 柴[①]

王 维

空山不见人，
但闻人语响。
返景入深林[②]，
复照青苔上。

① 鹿柴：柴同“寨(zhài)”，木栅栏。鹿柴，地名。
② 返景：谓太阳落山时的回光。景，阳光。

英汉对照
English-Chinese
中国文学宝库
Gems of Chinese Literature
古代文学系列
Classical Literature

The Luan Family Rapids

Wang Wei

In spattering autumn rain
Over the rocks the swirling rapids plunge;
The leaping water sprinkles all around,
Startled into flight, the white egret alights again.

栾家濑[1]

王　维

飒飒秋雨中[2]，
浅浅石溜泻[3]。
跳波自相溅，
白鹭惊复下。

① 濑(lài)：指浅水从沙石上急速流过之处。
② 飒飒(sà)：风声或雨声。这里指雨声。
③ 浅浅：(jiān)：水流声。石溜：石上的急流。

The Bamboo Lodge

Wang Wei

Seated alone by shadowy bamboos,
I strum my lyre and laugh aloud;
None knows that I am here, deep in the woods;
Only the bright moon comes to shine on me.

竹里馆

王　维

独坐幽篁里①，
弹琴复长啸②。
深林人不知，
明月来相照。

① 篁(huáng)：竹林。
② 长啸：啸，撮口作声，打口哨。

Hibiscus Valley

Wang Wei

Hibiscus high on the trees,
Flaunt red in the hills;
To this secluded valley no one comes,
Yet the flowers bloom and fall year after year.

辛夷坞[1]

王 维

木末芙蓉花[2]，
山中发红萼。
涧户寂无人，
纷纷开且落。

① 辛夷坞：地名。辛夷，一名木笔，落叶乔木，春天开花，有白紫两色，大如莲花，白者俗称玉兰。坞，四面高中间凹下的地方。

② 木末句：木末，树梢。辛夷花像莲花（一名芙蓉），却开在树枝头，所以说是“木末芙蓉花”，并非指木芙蓉。

英汉对照
English-Chinese
中国文学宝库
Gems of Chinese Literature
古代文学系列
Classical Literature

Seeing Yuan the Second Off on a Mission to Anxi

Wang Wei

A morning shower in Weicheng has settled the light dust;
The willows by the hostel are fresh and green;
Come, drink one more cup of wine.
West of the pass you will meet no more old friends.

送元二使安西①

王　维

渭城朝雨浥轻尘②，
客舍青青柳色新③。
劝君更尽一杯酒，
西出阳关无故人④。

① 元二：未详何人。安西：指安西都护府，今新疆库车县境。
② 渭城：秦都咸阳。浥(yì)：沾湿。
③ 客舍：旅馆。
④ 阳关：关名，今甘肃西部。

The Sichuan Road

Li Bai

What heights!
It is easier to climb to Heaven
Than take the Sichuan Road.
Long ago Can Cong and Yu Fu founded the kingdom of
Shu;
Forty-eight thousand years went by,
Yet no road linked it with the land of Qin[1].
Westward from Taibai Mountain[2] only birds
Wander to the summit of Mount Emei[3]

---

① Shu, the old name for Western Sichuan, was conquered by the kingdom of Qin in 316 BC.
② A mountain west of the capital, Chang'an.
③ A mountain in Western Sichuan.

蜀道难

李 白

噫吁嚱①，
危乎高哉②！
蜀道之难，
难于上青天。
蚕丛及鱼凫③，
开国何茫然④。
尔来四万八千岁，
不与秦塞通人烟⑤。
西当太白有鸟道⑥，
可以横绝峨眉巅⑦。

① 噫(yī 一)吁(xū 虚)嚱(xī 希)：惊叹声。
② 危乎高哉：高啊高啊。
③ 蚕丛、鱼凫(fú 浮)：传说中古蜀国的两个先王。
④ 茫然：是说蜀国开国久远，其事迹渺茫难详。
⑤ "尔来"二句：是说蜀、秦两地长期隔绝。尔来，指从开国以来。四万八千岁，形容时间久远，未必实数。秦塞(sài 赛)，犹言秦地。秦中自古称四塞之国。
⑥ 太白：山名，在今陕西省眉县东南。鸟道：鸟飞的径道。
⑦ 峨眉：山名，在今四川省峨眉县西南。

But not until brave men had perished in the great landslide[1]
Were bridges hooked together in the air
And a path hacked through the rocks.
Above, high peaks turn back the sun's chariot drawn by six dragons;
Below, the charging waves are caught in whirlpools;
Not even yellow cranes dare fly this way,
Monkeys cannot leap those gorges.
At Green Mud Ridge the path winds back and forth,
With nine twists for every hundred steps.
Touching the stars, the traveller looks up and gasps,
Then sinks down, clutching his heart, to groan aloud.
Friend, when will you return from this westward journey?
This is a fearful way. You cannot cross these cliffs.

① There is a legend that King Hui of Qin promised his five daughters to the prince of Shu. Five brave men were sent to fetch them. On the way back they met a huge serpent which fled into a cave. When they tried to pull it out, the mountain crumbled and the men and princesses perished. Since then a rocky path linked the two kingdoms.

地崩山摧壮士死①,
然后天梯石栈相钩连②。
上有六龙回日之高标③,
下有冲波逆折之回川④。
黄鹤之飞尚不得过,
猿猱欲度愁攀援⑤。
青泥何盘盘⑥,
百步九折萦岩峦⑦。
扪参历井仰胁息⑧,
以手抚膺坐长叹。
问君西游何时还⑨,
畏途巉岩不可攀⑩。

---

① "地崩"句:据《华阳国志·蜀志》所载,秦惠王知蜀王好色,特送他五个美女。蜀王派五个大力士去迎接。回到梓潼时,见一大蛇钻入山洞中,五力士共同抓住蛇尾往外拉,忽然间山崩地裂,把五个壮士和美女全埋在底下,山分成了五岭。秦王因此打通了蜀地。

② 天梯:形容山路陡峭,如登天的梯子。石栈(zhàn 站):在高山险绝处凿石架木而成的道路。

③ 六龙:古代神话记载,给日神赶车的羲和,每天驾着六条神龙拉的车子,载着太阳在空中运行。回日:是说太阳车至此要迂回绕道而过。高标:指蜀中的最高峰。

④ 逆折:往回倒流。

⑤ 猱(náo 挠):猿类动物,体矮小,攀缘树木轻捷如飞。

⑥ 青泥:岭名,在今陕西略阳县西北,为当时入蜀要道。盘盘:纡回曲折的样子。

⑦ 岩峦:山峰。

⑧ 扪(mén 门):抚摸。参(shēn 身)、井:均为星宿名。"扪参历井"是说由秦入蜀好似摸到参星,擦过井宿。

⑨ 君:此指入蜀的友人。西游:指入蜀。

⑩ 畏途:艰险可怕的道路。巉(chán 蝉)岩:险峻的山石。

The only living things are birds crying in ancient trees,
Male wooing female up and down the woods,
And the cuckoo, weary of empty hills,
Singing to the moon.
It is easier to cimb to heaven
Than take the Sichuan Road.
The mere telling of its perils blanches youthful cheeks.
Peak follows peak, each but a hand's breadth from the
  sky;
Dead pine trees hang head down into the chasms,
Torrents and waterfalls outroar each other,
Pounding the cliffs and boiling over rocks,
Booming like thunder through a thousand caverns.
What takes you, traveller, this long, weary way
So filled with danger?
Sword Pass① is steep and narrow.
One man could hold this pass against ten thousand;
And sometimes its defenders

---

① In northern Sichuan, on the route to Shaanxi where the kingdom of Qin was.

但见悲鸟号古木①，
雄飞雌从绕林间。
又闻子规啼夜月，
愁空山②。
蜀道之难，
难于上青天，
使人听此凋朱颜③。
连峰去天不盈尺，
枯松倒挂倚绝壁④。
飞湍瀑流争喧豗⑤，
砯崖转石万壑雷⑥。
其险也如此，
嗟尔远道之人胡为乎来哉⑦！
剑阁峥嵘而崔嵬⑧，
一夫当关，
万夫莫开。
所守或匪亲，

---

① 号：悲鸣。
② 子规：即杜鹃鸟，又名杜宇。
③ 凋朱颜：容颜失色。
④ 倚：依。
⑤ 飞湍(tuān)：如飞的急流。喧豗(hūi 灰)：喧闹声。
⑥ “砯(pēng 烹)崖”句：是说急流在一道道山沟中奔腾的冲击，使石翻滚，发出雷鸣般的声响。砯，水击岩石声，此作动词冲击解。
⑦ 胡为乎：为什么。
⑧ 剑阁：大、小剑山之间的一条三十里长的栈道，在今四川剑阁县北。峥嵘：高峻的样子。崔嵬(wéi 围)：高险崎岖。

Are not mortal men but wolves and jackals.
By day we dread the savage tiger,
By night the serpent,
Sharp-fanged sucker of blood
Who chops men down like stalks of hemp.
The City of Brocade[1] may be a pleasant place,
But it is best to seek your home.
For it is easier to climb to Heaven
Than take the Sichuan Road.
I gaze into the west, and sigh.

① A name for Chengdu, the capital of Shu.

化为狼与豺①。
朝避猛虎，
夕避长蛇，
磨牙吮血，
杀人如麻。
锦城虽云乐②，
不如早还家。
蜀道之难，
难于上青天，
侧身西望长咨嗟③！

① “一夫”四句：西晋张载《剑阁铭》：“一人荷戟，万夫趑(zī 资)趄(jū 居；犹豫不进)。形胜之地，匪亲弗居。”此化用其语，以状剑阁的险要。或匪亲，如果不是可信赖的人。匪，同“非”。一说狼、豺及下两句的猛虎、长蛇，均比喻分裂者或叛乱者。

② 锦城：锦官城的简称，即成都，蜀国的都城。

③ 咨(zī 资)嗟(jiē 皆)：叹息。

Travelling Is Hard

Li Bai

Clear wine in golden goblets, ten thousand cash a cup,
And costly delicacies on jade platters.
Yet I spurn drinking and toss away my chopsticks,
Sword in hand, restless, I wonder what to do.
I want to cross the Yellow River, but it's ice-bound;
I want to climb the Taihang Mountains, but they're snow-covered.
So idly I fish by a limpid stream ①,
Dreaming of sailing towards the sun②.
Travelling is hard! Travelling is hard!
So many crossroads; which to choose?
One day I'll skim the waves, blown by the wind,
With sails hoisted high, across the vast ocean.

---

① Lü Shang used to fish by the Wei River before he met King Wen of Zhou and helped him to conquer the Shangs.

② Yi Yin, before he was discovered by King Tang of Shang, dreamed that he was sailing in a barge towards the sun.

行路难(其一)

李　白

金樽清酒斗十千，
玉盘珍羞值万钱①。
停杯投箸不能食，
拔剑四顾心茫然②。
欲渡黄河冰塞川，
将登太行雪满山。
闲来垂钓坐溪上，
忽复乘舟梦日边③。
行路难！行路难！
多歧路，今安在④？
乘风破浪会有时，
直挂云帆济沧海⑤。

① 斗十千：一斗酒价值十千钱，极言酒美。羞：同"馐"，美味食品。
② 箸(zhù 铸)：筷子。
③ 垂钓坐溪上：《史记·齐太公世家》记载，吕尚九十岁时垂钓于磻溪，得遇周文王。梦日边：传说伊尹在将受到成汤的征聘时，梦见乘船经过日月旁边。这两句用吕尚、伊尹的故事，暗示人生遭遇变化无常。
④ 安在：在哪里。
⑤ 乘风破浪：南朝宋时的宗悫曾用："乘长风破万里浪"来比喻在政治上施展抱负。济：渡。

A Visit to Sky-Mother Mountain in a Dream

Li Bai

Seafarers tell of fairy isles;
Lost among mist and waves.
But the men of Yue[1] speak of Sky-Mother Mountain
Showing herself through rifts in shimmering clouds.
Sky-Mother soars to heaven, spans the horizon,
Towers over the Five Peaks[2] and the Scarlet Fortress;
While Sky-Terrace, four hundred and eighty thousand
feet high,
Staggers southeastward before it.
So, longing in my dreams for Wu and Yue,
One night I flew over Mirror Lake under the moon;
The moon cast my shadow on the water

---

① The land of Yue lay in what is now Zhejiang Province, the home of the famous mountains: Sky-Mother, Scarlet Fortress and Sky-Terrace.

② Five high mountains in China: Mount Tai, Mount Hua, Mount Heng in the south, Mount Heng in the north and Mount Song.

梦游天姥吟留别

李　白

海客谈瀛洲，
烟涛微茫信难求①。
越人语天姥，
云霞明灭或可睹②。
天姥连天向天横，
势拔五岳掩赤城③。
天台四万八千丈，
对此欲倒东南倾④。
我欲因之梦吴越，
一夜飞度镜湖月⑤。
湖月照我影，

① 海客：航海的人。瀛洲：古代传说东海中有蓬莱、方丈、瀛洲三座仙山。微茫：模糊不清的样子。信：确实。

② 越：今浙江省一带地方。语：谈论。云霞明灭：指天姥山在云霞中时隐时现。

③ 拔：超拔。五岳：我国五座大名山的总称，即东岳泰山，西岳华山，南岳衡山，北岳恒山，中岳嵩山。掩：盖过。赤城：山名，在今浙江省天台县北。

④ 天台：山名，在今浙江省天台县北。此：指天姥山。这两句是说，那四万八千丈高的天台山对着天姥山，像是要拜倒一样地向着东南方向倾倒。

⑤ 之：这，指代越人对天姥山的谈论。吴越：今江苏省南部及浙江一带地方。镜湖：又名鉴湖或庆湖，在今浙江省绍兴县南。

And travelled with me all the way to Shanxi.
The lodge of Lord Xie[1] still remained
Where green waters swirled and the cry of apes was shrill;
Donning the shoes of Xie,
I climbed the dark ladder of clouds.
Midway, I saw the sun rise from the sea,
Heard the Cock of Heaven crow[2].
And my path twisted through a thousand crags,
Enchanted by flowers I leaned against a rock,
And suddenly all was dark.
Growls of bears and snarls of dragons echoed
Among the rocks and streams;
The deep forest appalled me, I shrank from the lowering cliffs;
Dark were the clouds, heavy with rain;
Waters boiled into misty spray;
Lightning flashed; thunder roared;
Peaks tottered, boulders crashed;
And the stone gate of a great cavern

---

① Xie Lingyun, a Jin-dynasty poet who was fond of mountaineering and made himself special hobnailed shoes for climbing.

② According to Chinese mythology, this cock roosted on a great tree in the southeast. When the sun rose it crowed, and all the cocks in the world followed suit.

送我到剡溪①。
谢公宿处今尚在，
渌水荡漾清猿啼②。
脚着谢公屐，
身登青云梯③。
半壁见海日，
空中闻天鸡④。
千岩万转路不定，
迷花倚石忽已暝⑤。
熊咆龙吟殷岩泉，
慄深林兮惊层巅⑥。
云青青兮欲雨，
水澹澹兮生烟⑦。
列缺霹雳，
丘峦崩摧⑧。
洞天石扉，

---

① 剡(Shàn 善)溪：在今浙江省嵊(shèng 圣)县南，即曹娥江的上游。

② 谢公宿处：指南北朝宋代诗人谢灵运当年游览剡溪时的投宿处。清猿啼：清亮的猿啼声。

③ 谢公屐(jī 积)：是谢灵运特制的一种专供游山用的木鞋，底下装有活动的齿，上山时抽去前齿，下山时抽去后齿。青云梯：高峻陡峭的山路，好像是登攀青天的梯子。

④ 半壁：半山腰。海日：海中升起的太阳。闻天鸡：指天亮了。《述异记》说我国东南边有桃都山，山上长着一种名桃都的大树，树上有天鸡，每天早晨，阳光一照到桃都树上，天鸡就叫起来，于是天下的鸡都跟着叫起来。

⑤ 暝(míng 明)：日落，天黑。

⑥ 殷(yǐn 引)：震动。层巅：层层的山峰。

⑦ 云青青：形容云层的浓厚。水澹澹(dàn 淡)：形容水波荡漾。

⑧ 列缺：闪电。霹雳：雷。

Yawned open.
Below me, a bottomless void of blue,
Sun and moon gleaming on terraces of silver and gold;
With rainbows for garments, and winds for horses,
The lords of the clouds descended, a mighty host.
Phoenixes circled the chariots, tigers played zithers,
As the immortals went by, rank upon rank.
My heart was seized by fear and wonder,
And waking with a start I cried out,
For nothing was there except my mat and pillow —
Gone was the world of mists and clouds.
And so with the pleasure of this life;
And pass, as water flows eastward.
I leave you, friend—when shall I return?
I shall pasture white stags among green peaks
And ride to visit mountains famed in legend.
Would you have me bow my head before mighty princes,
Forgetting all the joy of my heart?

訇然中开①。
青冥浩荡不见底，
日月照耀金银台②。
霓为衣兮风为马，
云之君兮纷纷而来下③。
虎鼓瑟兮鸾回车，
仙之人兮列如麻④。
忽魂悸以魄动，
恍惊起而长嗟⑤。
惟觉时之枕席，
失向来之烟霞⑥。
世间行乐亦如此，
古来万事东流水⑦。
别君去兮何时还？
且放白鹿青崖间，
须行即骑访名山⑧。
安能摧眉折腰事权贵⑨，
使我不得开心颜！

---

① 洞天：神仙的居处。石扉(fēi 非)：石门。訇(hōng 烘)然：巨大的响声。
② 青冥：青色的天空。金银台：用金银装饰的仙宫楼台。
③ 云之君：云神。
④ 回车：回转车子，即驾着车子。
⑤ 悸：惊怕。恍(huǎng 谎)：同"恍"，心神不定的样子。长嗟：长声叹息。
⑥ 觉：醒。向来：刚才。烟霞：指梦游中的幻境。
⑦ 亦如此：也如同梦中的景象变化莫测。
⑧ 君：指在山东漫游时结交的朋友。白鹿：传说中神仙的一种代步的神兽。
⑨ 摧眉折腰：低眉弯腰。事：侍奉，伺候。

英汉对照
English-Chinese
中国文学宝库
Gems of Chinese Literature
古代文学系列
Classical Literature

Seeing Meng Haoran Off from Yellow Crane Tower

Li Bai

At Yellow Crane Tower in the west
My old friend says farewell;
In the mist and flowers of spring
He goes down to Yangzhou[1];
Lonely sail, distant shadow,
Vanish in blue emptiness;
All I see is the great river
Flowing into the far horizon.

① Also known as Guangling at that time.

黄鹤楼送孟浩然之广陵

李　白

故人西辞黄鹤楼，
烟花三月下扬州①。
孤帆远影碧空尽②，
唯见长江天际流。

① 西辞：黄鹤楼在广陵之西，孟浩然由西去东，所以说“西辞”。烟花：指桃花盛开的绚烂景色。
② 碧空尽：在碧色的天空中消逝了。

英汉对照
English-Chinese
中国文学宝库
Gems of Chinese Literature
古代文学系列
Classical Literature

Evening Song(Ⅲ)

Li Bai

Chang'an under a new moon, and I in the evening
listen to the sound of many women beating clothes by the water.

An autumn wind blows and I know well
that many a woman feels its chill, and is anxious for
her husband, fighting in the far Northwest —
then she thinks, "I wonder when the war will end,
so that he will no longer need to fight."

子夜吴歌[①] (其三)

李 白

长安一片月，
万户捣衣声。
秋风吹不尽，
总是玉关情[②]。
何日平胡虏，
良人罢远征[③]？

① 子夜吴歌：六朝乐府歌曲名。内容多写女子思念情人的哀怨。
② 玉关：玉门关。
③ 良人：丈夫。

英汉对照
English-Chinese
中国文学宝库
Gems of Chinese Literature
古代文学系列
Classical Literature

Evening Song(Ⅳ)

Li Bai

Tomorrow a courier will gallop
swiftly west, and will take from her
a gift;

so preparing it she sits
through the night — a soldier's
padded coat — and into its stitching
she puts her heart.

Fingers freeze so that movement
becomes difficult; to grasp
the ice-cold scissors painful;

Yet before dawn sewing is finished
and hopefully she hands it to relay riders
to carry all the long way to Lintao;
wondering anxiously how many days it will be
before he wears her handiwork.

子夜吴歌(其四)

李　白

明朝驿使发，
一夜絮征袍①。
素手抽针冷，
那堪把剪刀。
裁缝寄远道，
几日到临洮②？

① 驿使：为政府传送书信和物件的使者。
② 临洮：地名，在今甘肃省境内。

英汉对照
English-Chinese
中国文学宝库
Gems of Chinese Literature
古代文学系列
Classical Literature

Thoughts in Spring

Li Bai

The grass of Yan is green silk,
Dark hang the mulberry boughs of Qin.
While you, my lord, are longing to return,
Your handmaiden is breaking her heart at home.
Ah, why does the spring wind, a stranger,
Part the curtains of my bed?

春 思

李 白

燕草如碧丝，
秦桑低绿枝[1]。
当君怀归日，
是妾断肠时。
春风不相识，
何事入罗帏？

英汉对照
English-Chinese
中国文学宝库
Gems of Chinese Literature
古代文学系列
Classical Literature

① 燕：指燕地（今河北北部、辽宁西南部一带），是诗中女子的丈夫征戍的地方。秦，指秦地（今陕西），是诗中女子所居之地。

Ascending Taibai Peak

Li Bai

Ascending Taibai Peak from the west,
I reach the summit in the sunset.
The morning star speaks to me.
Opening the gate of Heaven.
I wish to go with the wind,
Emerge from the floating clouds,
Raise my hand to touch the moon
And travel over all the mountains.
Once I have left Wugong,
When shall I return again?

登太白峰

李　白

西上太白峰，
夕阳穷登攀[①]。
太白与我语，
为我开天关[②]。
愿乘泠风去，
直出浮云间。
举手可近月，
前行若无山。
一别武功去，
何时复更还？

① 太白峰：即太白山。在今陕西省兴平县南。
② “太白句”中的太白：大约是指太白星，即金星。

英汉对照
English-Chinese
中国文学宝库
Gems of Chinese Literature
古代文学系列
Classical Literature

Invitation to Wine

Li Bai

Do you not see the Yellow River come from the sky,
Rushing into the sea and ne'er come back?
Do you not see the mirrors bright in chambers high
Grieve o'er your snow-white hair though once it was silk-
black?
When hopes are won, oh! drink your fill in high delight,
And never leave your wine-cup empty in moonlight!
Heaven has made us talents, we're not made in vain.
A thousand gold coins spent, more will turn up again.
Kill a cow, cook a sheep and let us merry be,
And drink three hundred cupfuls of wine in high glee!
Dear friends of mine,
Cheer up, cheer up!
I invite you to wine.
Do not put down your cup!
I will sing you a song, please hear,
O hear! lend me a willing ear!
What difference will rare and costly dishes make?
I only want to get drunk and never to wake.
How many great men were forgotten through the ages?
But great drinkers are more famous than sober sages.

将进酒[1]

李 白

君不见黄河之水天上来，
奔流到海不复回！
又不见高堂明镜悲白发，
朝如青丝暮成雪！
人生得意须尽欢，
莫使金樽空对月。
天生我材必有用，
千金散尽还复来。
烹羊宰牛且为乐，
会须一饮三百杯。
岑夫子，丹丘生，
将进酒，杯莫停[2]。
与君歌一曲，
请君为我倾耳听。
钟鼓馔玉不足贵，
但愿长醉不复醒[3]。
古来圣贤皆寂寞，
惟有饮者留其名。

① “将进酒”：原是汉乐府鼓吹铙歌的曲调。
② 岑夫子：李白的好友岑勋。
③ 馔(zhuàn)玉：形容食品精美。

The Prince of Poets feast'd in his palace at will,
Drank wine at ten thousand a cask and laughed his fill.
A host should not complain of money he is short,
To drink with you I will sell things of any sort.
My fur coat worth a thousand coins of gold
And my flower-dappled horse may be sold
To buy good wine that we may drown the woes age old.

陈王昔时宴平乐，
斗酒十千恣欢谑①。
主人何为言少钱，
径须沽取对君酌。
五花马，千金裘，
呼儿将出换美酒，
与尔同销万古愁。

① 陈王：即三国时的诗人曹植。

A Farewell to Li Yun in the Xie Tiao Pavilion

Li Bai

Yesterday has passed and gone beyond recall;
Today worries and sorrows assail my mind.
Gazing at wild geese flying in the autumn wind,
Let us drink our fill in this high pavilion.
Here is one who writes with great scholarship;
His spirited style and poems compare with Xie Tiao.
Our lofty ambitions soar high;
Seeking to reach the moon in the sky.
Cut water with a sword, the water flows on;
Quench sorrow with wine, the sorrow increases.
In our lifetime, our wishes are unfulfilled;
Tomorrow, hair unbound, we'll sail away in a boat.

宣州谢朓楼饯别校书叔云[1]

李 白

弃我去者，
昨日之日不可留；
乱我心者，
今日之日多烦忧。
长风万里送秋雁，
对此可以酣高楼。
蓬莱文章建安骨，
中间小谢又清发[2]。
俱怀逸兴壮思飞，
欲上青天览明月。
抽刀断水水更流，
举杯消愁愁更愁。
人生在世不称意，
明朝散发弄扁舟。

① 宣州：今安徽宣城县。云，李云，李白族叔。
② 蓬莱：海上神山名，这里指李云。小谢：指谢朓。

英汉对照
English-Chinese
中国文学宝库
Gems of Chinese Literature
古代文学系列
Classical Literature

To Wang Lun

Li Bai

I'm on board; we're about to sail,
When there's stamping and singing on shore;
Peach Blossom Pool is a thousand feet deep,
Yet not so deep, Wang Lun, as your love for me.

赠汪伦[1]

李 白

李白乘舟将欲行，
忽闻岸上踏歌声。
桃花潭水深千尺[2]，
不及汪伦送我情。

英汉对照
English-Chinese
中国文学宝库
Gems of Chinese Literature
古代文学系列
Classical Literature

① 汪伦：当地的村民。
② 桃花潭：在今安徽省泾县西南。

Departure from Baidicheng at Dawn

Li Bai

In the bright dawn clouds I left Baidicheng;
A thousand *li* to Jiangling only takes a day.
I hear the incessant cry of monkeys from the banks;
My light barge has passed countless folds of hills.

早发白帝城①

李　白

朝辞白帝彩云间，
千里江陵一日还。
两岸猿声啼不住，
轻舟已过万重山。

英汉对照
English-Chinese
中国文学宝库
Gems of Chinese Literature
古代文学系列
Classical Literature

① 白帝城：在今四川奉节县东。

Looking at the Moon

Li Bai

Looking across the desert to Tianshan Mountains
and at a moon that seems to float over a sea of cloud,
steppe and desert over which
the wind blows unceasingly,
whistling around the towers of Yu Men Guan;

I think of the bitterness of the Bai Deng Road
and of the tribesmen around
the shores of Lake Kokonor
ever pressing against us.

It is an old story, that from the battlefield
no man ever returns; so the soldiers gaze
back at the frontier regions

all with the longing to return home
written in the gaunt lines of their faces.

And I think of the towers in our distant homes
where our loved ones will be standing and sighing
with no answering sound coming from the stillness.

关山月[1]

李 白

明月出天山，
苍茫云海间[2]。
长风几万里，
吹度玉门关。
汉下白登道，
胡窥青海湾[3]。
由来征战地，
不见有人还。
戍客望边色，
思归多苦颜。
高楼当此夜，
叹息未应闲。

① “关山月”：是乐府旧题，内容多写离别的哀伤。
② 天山：指今甘肃省西北部的祁连山。
③ 白登：山名，在今山西大同东。青海：湖名，在今青海省东北部。

Thoughts in the Silent Night

Li Bai

Beside my bed a pool of light —
Is it hoarfrost on the ground?
I lift my eyes and see the moon,
I bend my head and think of home.

静夜思

李　白

床前明月光，
疑是地上霜。
举头望明月，
低头思故乡。

Watching the Waterfall at Lushan

Li Bai

In sunshine Censer Peak breathes purple vapor,
Far off hangs the cataract, a stream upended;
Down it cascades a sheer three thousand feet —
As if the Silver River were falling from Heaven!

望庐山瀑布(其二)

李　白

日照香炉生紫烟，
遥看瀑布挂前川。
飞流直下三千尺，
疑是银河落九天。

英汉对照
English-Chinese
中国文学宝库
Gems of Chinese Literature
古代文学系列
Classical Literature

On Hearing a Flute Melody in the Borderlands

Gao Shi

Snow has thawed in the borderlands, grazing horses returned,
A flute melody hovers amid moonlit watchtowers.
Where is the tune of *Fallen Plum Blossom* played?
It wafts through the borderlands on the night wind.

塞上听吹笛

高　适

霜净胡天牧马还，
月明羌笛戍楼间①。
借问梅花何处落②，
风吹一夜满关山。

① “霜净”两句说，霜后的边塞，秋高气爽，在牧马已还的明月之夜，士兵们吹起悦耳的羌笛。
② 梅花：《梅花落》曲的简称。

Song of Yan

Gao Shi

In the twenty-sixth year[1] of the Kaiyuan reign, a gentleman who had come back from Chancellor Zhang's[2] mission to the frontier showed me his "Song of Yan", inspired by the war and garrison life, I composed this verse in reply.

The smoke and dust of war roll in the northeast,
The general leaves home to smash the tottering foe.
A true man is born to set great store by gallantry,
The emperor has deigned exceptional graces to him.
Beating drums and gongs the army march to Yuguan Pass[3],
Its standards and flags winding along Jieshi Hill.[4]
Field officers urgent dispatches speed across the desert,
Tartar chief's hunting fire sets Wolf Mountain[5] ablaze,
A desolate scene stretches to the farthest borderland,

---

① AD 738.

② Zhang Shougui(? -AD 739), once a meritorious general and high-ranking court official but later demoted for his false report of the military situation.

③ Shanhai Pass at present Linyu County, Hebei Province.

④ In present Changli County, Hebei.

⑤ Langjuxu Mountain in the northwest of present Inner Mongolia Autonomous Region.

燕歌行 并序

高　适

开元二十六年①，客有从御史大夫张公② 出塞而还者，作《燕歌行》以示适，感征戍之事，因而和焉。

汉家烟尘在东北，
汉将辞家破残贼。
男儿本自重横行，
天子非常赐颜色。
摐金伐鼓下榆关③，
旌旆逶迤碣石间④。
校尉羽书飞瀚海，
单于猎火照狼山。
山川萧条极边土，

① 公元738年。
② 张公：指张守珪，开元二十一年任幽州长史，二十二年以功拜辅国大将军、右羽林大将军兼御史大夫。
③ 榆关：山海关。
④ 碣石：山名，在今河北省昌黎县东。

With Tartar cavalry running amuck like a violent storm.
Half of the soldiers have laid down their lives in battle,
In the command camp pretty girls still sing and dance.
In the vast desert, grasses wither in late autumn,
In the isolated city, combatants are sparse at sunset.
Obliged to imperial bounty but always belittling the foe,
The forts remain besieged despite all-out efforts.
Mailed fighters at distant garrison have toiled long,
Their wives must be shedding tears for the separation.
In the south of the city young women are nearly heartbroken,
To the north of Ji[①] the marchers turn their heads in vain.
The plight on the borderland is hard to pull through,
In the remotest region there is nothing but desolation.
Battle clouds redolent of death linger all day long,
Dreary watch-beatings regularly permeate the chilly night.
Looking at the white blades dripping with blood,
Who can say the fallen fighters ever craved military merits?
Have you not seen the arduous fights on the battlefield?
Up to now people still cherish the memory of General Li![②]

---

① Referring to the Northeast of China. Ji was a Tang-dynasty prefecture with jurisdiction over a few counties near present Tianjin, Hebei.

② Li Guang(? -119 BC), a famous commander of Western Han Dynasty.

胡骑凭陵杂风雨。
战士军前半死生，
美人帐下犹歌舞。
大漠穷秋塞草衰，
孤城落日斗兵稀。
身当恩遇恒轻敌，
力尽关山未解围。
铁衣远戍辛勤久，
玉箸应啼别离后。
少妇城南欲断肠，
征人蓟北空回首①。
边庭飘飖那可度，
绝域苍茫更何有？
杀气三时作阵云，
寒声一夜传刁斗。
相看白刃血纷纷，
死节从来岂顾勋？
君不见沙场争战苦，
至今犹忆李将军②！

① 蓟(jì 季)北：指蓟门以北地区。
② 李将军：指汉代名将李广，他曾在右北平(今河北省北部)一带抵御匈奴。

Song of Yingzhou[1]

Gao Shi

Yingzhou youngsters are quite familiar with the campaign,
In fluffy fox furs they hunt in the suburbs of the town.
A thousand cups of strong wine would not make them drunk,
Tartar boys in early teens are good at horseback riding.

---

① A Tang-dynasty border town around present Chaoyang, Liaoning.

营州歌

高　适

营州少年厌原野①，
狐裘蒙茸猎城下②。
虏酒千锺不醉人，
胡儿十岁能骑马。

英汉对照
English-Chinese
中国文学宝库
Gems of Chinese Literature
古代文学系列
Classical Literature

① 厌原野：熟习于原野生活。
② 狐裘：狐皮袍子。蒙茸：毛茸茸。

The Army Carts

Du Fu

Carts rumbling, horses neighing,
Men march with bows and arrows at their waists;
Parents, wives and children are there to see them off,
And Xianyang Bridge is swallowed up in dust;
Stamping and clutching the men's clothes, blocking the road, they weep;
The sound of weeping rises to the clouds.
In answer to a passerby
The marchers say, "We're conscripts once again!
At fifteen some of us went north to guard the Yellow River;
Now forty, we are being sent to open waste land in the west.
When we left, the headman bound our head-cloths on;
White-haired and just home, we are off to the frontier again!
Seas of blood have been shed at the frontier,

兵车行

杜　甫

车辚辚，马萧萧①，
行人弓箭各在腰②。
耶娘妻子走相送。
尘埃不见咸阳桥③。
牵衣顿足拦道哭，
哭声直上干云霄④。
道旁过者问行人，
行人但云点行频⑤。
或从十五北防河，
便至四十西营田⑥。
去时里正与裹头⑦，
归来头白还戍边。
边庭流血成海水，

① 辚(lín 林)辚：车辆走动声。萧萧：马鸣声。
② 行人：指被征出发的战士。
③ 尘埃句：是说沿路灰尘弥漫，咸阳桥也看不见了。
④ 干：冲上。
⑤ 但云：只说。点行频：征调频繁。点行，按户籍点招壮丁。
⑥ “或从”二句是说，有的人十五岁起就远戍西北，直到四十岁还在屯田。
⑦ 里正：里长。与裹头：替壮丁裹扎头巾。说明应征壮丁之年幼。

英汉对照
English-Chinese
中国文学宝库
Gems of Chinese Literature
古代文学系列
Classical Literature

Yet still the emperor seeks to swell his realm.
It's said, in two hundred districts east of the Pass
Thousands of villages grow thick with brambles;
Even where sturdy women plough and hoe,
The crops are straggling in the ragged fields;
Since we of the northwest are seasoned fighters,
We are driven like dogs or hens.
You, sir, may show concern,
But how dare we soldiers complain?
Yet only this very winter
Troops west of the Pass had no rest;
The magistrate is plaguing us for taxes,
But where are taxes to come from?
We know now it is bad to bear sons,
Better to have daughters;
For a girl can be married to a next-door neighbour,
But a boy will perish like the grass in the field.
Have you not seen, beside Lake Kokonor,
Bleached bones, unburied from ancient times?
There new ghosts curse their fate and old ghosts wail;
In darkness and in rain you hear their sobbing."

武皇开边意未已①。
君不闻汉家山东二百州②，
千村万落生荆杞。
纵有健妇把锄犁，
禾生陇亩无东西③。
况复秦兵耐苦战④，
被驱不异犬与鸡。
长者虽有问，
役夫敢申恨？
且如今年冬，
未休关西卒⑤。
县官急索租，
租税从何出？
信知生男恶，
反是生女好；
生女犹得嫁比邻，
生男埋没随百草！
君不见青海头⑥，
古来白骨无人收。
新鬼烦冤旧鬼哭，
天阴雨湿声啾啾⑦！

---

① 武皇：汉武帝。此借指唐玄宗。开边：用武力扩张疆土。
② 汉家：借指唐朝。山东：指华山以东。二百州：唐代潼关以东有七道，共二百十七州，此约举整数。
③ “禾生”句：指庄稼种得不成行列。
④ 秦兵：关中兵。关中为古秦地。此指眼前被征调的壮丁。
⑤ 未休：指征调不止。关西卒：即“秦兵”。
⑥ 青海头：青海湖边，唐军与吐蕃常在此作战。
⑦ 啾(jiū 纠)啾：古人想像中的鬼哭声。

The Shihao Official

Du Fu

One sunset I came to the village of Shihao,
And shortly after there followed
An official, seizing conscripts.
In the courtyard of the peasant's house where I stayed,
An old man climbed quickly over the wall, and vanished.

To the door came his old wife to greet the official.
How fiercely he swore at her,
And how bitterly she cried!
"I have had three sons taken
To be soldiers at Yecheng.
Then came a letter, saying
Two had been killed, and that the third
Never knew which day he might die.
Now in this hut is left
None but a baby grandson
Whose mother still suckles him...
She cannot go out, as she has no clothes
To cover her nakedness.

石壕吏

杜　甫

暮投石壕村[①]，
有吏夜捉人。
老翁逾墙走，
老妇出门看[②]。
吏呼一何怒，
妇啼一何苦！
听妇前致词：
“三男邺城戍[③]，
一男附书至[④]，
二男新战死。
存者且偷生，
死者长已矣[⑤]！
室中更无人，
惟有乳下孙[⑥]。
有孙母未去，
出入无完裙。

① 投：投宿。石壕村：在今河南省陕县东。
② 逾(yú 余)：越。走：跑。
③ 邺城：即相州，今河南省安阳县。戍：守卫。
④ 附书：托人捎家信。
⑤ 长已矣：人死不能复生，永远完了。
⑥ 乳下孙：还在吃奶的孙儿。

英汉对照
English-Chinese
中国文学宝库
Gems of Chinese Literature
古代文学系列
Classical Literature

All I can do is to go back with you
To the battle at Heyang.
There I can cook for you,
Eevn though I am weak and old..."

Night wore on.
The sound of voices died away
Until there was left, coming from the hut,
Only the sobbing of the daughter-in-law.
At dawn I rose and left,
With only the old man
To bid me goodbye.

老妪力虽衰，
请从吏夜归①。
急应河阳役，
犹得备晨炊②。”
夜久语声绝，
如闻泣幽咽③。
天明登前途，
独与老翁别④。

① 妪(yù 玉)：年老的妇人。此为“听妇”自称。
② 河阳：孟津，在黄河北岸，今河南省孟县。
③ 夜久：夜深。泣幽咽：极为悲伤而吞声哭泣。
④ 登前途：登程上路。

英汉对照
English-Chinese
中国文学宝库
Gems of Chinese Literature
古代文学系列
Classical Literature

A Welcome Rain One Spring Night

Du Fu

A good rain knows its season
And comes when spring is here;
On the heels of the wind it slips secretly into the night,
Silent and soft, it moistens everything.
Now clouds hang black above the country roads,
A lone boat on the river sheds a glimmer of light;
At dawn we shall see splashes of rain-washed red —
Drenched, heavy blooms in the City of Brocade. ①

① Another name for Chengdu.

春夜喜雨

杜　甫

好雨知时节，
当春乃发生①。
随风潜入夜，
润物细无声。
野径云俱黑，
江船火独明②。
晓看红湿处，
花重锦官城③。

① 当春：正当春天需要雨的时候。
② 野径：田野间的道路。
③ 花重：花朵因饱含雨水而沉重。红湿：指花带雨水而湿。锦官城：今四川省成都市的别称。

My Thatched Hut Wrecked by the Autumn Wind

Du Fu

The eighth month and a mid-autumn gale
Tore off the three layers of my thatch;
Across the stream flew the straw to scatter the banks,
Caught high up on tall trees
Or fluttering down into the pools and ditches.
The village boys found a feeble old man easy game,
And robbed me to my face,
Openly lugging off armfuls through the bamboos,
Though I shouted till I was hoarse and my lips parched.
I went home then, leaning on my stick, and sighed.

Soon the wind fell and black clouds gathered,
The autumn sky grew dark as dusk came on;
My quilt after years of use is cold as iron,
With rents kicked in it by my spoiled, restless son;

茅屋为秋风所破歌

杜　甫

八月秋高风怒号，
卷我屋上三重茅①。
茅飞渡江洒江郊，
高者挂罥长林梢②，
下者飘转沉塘坳③。
南村群童欺我老无力，
忍能对面为盗贼④。
公然抱茅入竹去⑤，
唇焦口燥呼不得⑥，
归来倚杖自叹息。
俄顷风定云墨色⑦，
秋天漠漠向昏黑⑧。
布衾多年冷似铁，
娇儿恶卧踏里裂⑨。

① 三重茅：几层茅草，是虚指。
② 罥(juàn 绢)：挂。长：高。
③ 塘坳：低注积水处。
④ 忍能：怎忍心？
⑤ 竹：指竹林。
⑥ 呼不得：喝不住。
⑦ 俄顷：一会儿。
⑧ 漠漠：阴沉沉、灰蒙蒙的样子。
⑨ 恶卧：睡相不好。里：被里子。

英汉对照
English-Chinese
中国文学宝库
Gems of Chinese Literature
古代文学系列
Classical Literature

The roof, no patch of it dry, leaks over my bed
And the rain streams through like unending strands of
hemp;
Ever since the rebellion I have been losing sleep;
Wet through, how can I last out this long night till
dawn?

Oh, for a great mansion with ten thousand rooms
Where all the poor on earth could find welcome shelter,
Steady through every storm, secure as a mountain!
Ah, were such a building to spring up before me,
I would freeze to death in my wrecked hut well content.

床头屋漏无干处，
雨脚如麻未断绝。
自经丧乱少睡眠[1]，
长夜沾湿何由彻[2]！
安得广厦千万间，
大庇天下寒士俱欢颜[3]，
风雨不动安如山！
呜呼！何时眼前突兀见此屋[4]，
吾庐独破受冻死亦足！

① 丧乱：此指安史之乱。
② 何由彻：怎么才能挨到天亮。彻：彻晓。
③ 庇(bì 毕)：遮盖护住。
④ 突兀：高耸的样子，见：同"现"。

英汉对照
English-Chinese
中国文学宝库
Gems of Chinese Literature
古代文学系列
Classical Literature

Climbing the Yueyang Tower

Du Fu

I have long heard of Lake Dongting;
Now I ascend the Yueyang Tower.
It separates the lands of Wu and Chu,
One in the east, the other in the south.
The sun and moon seem to float there day and night.
I have heard nothing from my family and friends;
Growing old and ill, alone I sail in a barge.
War rages in the northern mountain passes;
Leaning on a balustrade I shed tears.

登岳阳楼

杜　甫

昔闻洞庭水，
今上岳阳楼。
吴楚东南坼，
乾坤日夜浮①。
亲朋无一字，
老病有孤舟。
戎马关山北，
凭轩涕泗流。

① 坼：裂开，指洞庭湖将吴与楚的疆域划分开。

Climbing a Terrace

Du Fu

Wind blusters high in the sky and monkeys wail;
Clear the islet with white sand where birds are wheeling;
Everywhere the leaves fall rustling from the trees,
While on for ever rolls the turbulent Yangtze.
All around is autumnal gloom and I, long from home,
A prey all my life to ill health, chimb the terrace alone;
Hating the hardships which have frosted my hair,
Sad that illness has made me give up the solace of wine.

登 高

杜 甫

风急天高猿啸哀，
渚清沙白鸟飞回。
无边落木萧萧下，
不尽长江滚滚来。
万里悲秋常作客，
百年多病独登台。
艰难苦恨繁霜鬓，
潦倒新停浊酒杯。

英汉对照
English-Chinese
中国文学宝库
Gems of Chinese Literature
古代文学系列
Classical Literature

The White Emperor's City

Du Fu

From the White Emperor's City clouds are drifting;
Below, rain pours down like a basin overturned;
Flood waters rush through the gorge, thunder battles with lightning;
Sun and moon grow dim among green trees and gray vines.
War-horses are not as content as horses at grass,
Of a thousand families only a hundred are left;
Widows ruined by cruel taxation are in despair,
Sobbing sounds on the autumn plain in every village.

白　帝

杜　甫

白帝城中云出门，
白帝城下雨翻盆。
高江急峡雷霆斗，
古木苍藤日月昏。
戎马不如归马逸，
千家今有百家存。
哀哀寡妇诛求尽①，
恸哭秋原何处村？

英汉对照
English-Chinese
中国文学宝库
Gems of Chinese Literature
古代文学系列
Classical Literature

① “哀哀”句：官府将寡妇家搜刮尽净。

Thoughts When Travelling at Night

Du Fu

Between soft, grassy banks in the light breeze
A lone, tall-masted boat sails through the night;
Stars hang low above the wide, flat plain,
And up rides the moon as the mighty river flows on.
Since I have not in truth won fame by writing,
In old age and illness I should retire from office.
Drifting along, to what can I liken myself?
A lonely beach gull between heaven and earth.

旅夜书怀

杜　甫

细草微风岸，
危樯独夜舟。
星垂平野阔，
月涌大江流。
名岂文章著？
官应老病休。
飘飘何所似，
天地一沙鸥。

Dreaming of Li Bai(I)

Du Fu

Were we parted by death, I might swallow my grief,
But to be parted in life is pain unending;
South of the Yangtze is a malarial region,
And still no news of the exile;
Yet you appear, my old friend, in my dreams,
Which shows how you fill my thoughts.
But was this the spirit of a living man?
So far away, there is no way of knowing!
Through the green maple forest you came,
Returning by dark passes and fortresses.
Caught in a net,
How did you take wings to fly?
When the dying moon lights the rafters of my room
I can almost see your face reflected there.
Deep the river, wild the waves;
Beware of dragons and serpents!

梦李白(其一)

杜 甫

死别已吞声，
生别常恻恻。
江南瘴疠地，
逐客无消息。
故人入我梦，
明我长相忆。
恐非平生魂，
路远不可测。
魂来枫林青，
魂返关塞黑。
今君在罗网，
何以有羽翼？
落月满屋梁，
犹疑照颜色。
水深波浪阔，
无使蛟龙得。

英汉对照
English-Chinese
中国文学宝库
Gems of Chinese Literature
古代文学系列
Classical Literature

Dreaming of Li Bai(Ⅱ)

Du Fu

All day the clouds drift by;
Too long has the wanderer been away.
These three nights I have dreamed of you
And seen the love in your heart;
But every time you took a hasty leave,
For the way was rough, the journey hard,
Many the storms on rivers and on lakes
And easy for a small boat to capsize;
So off you went, rubbing your hoary head,
Like one who has failed in a lifelong ambition.
Officials in all their state throng the capital,
You alone are careworn, passed over.
Who speaks of justice when Heaven casts its net?
My friend in his old age is caught in the toils.
His name will live for centuries to come,
But fame is little comfort after death.

梦李白(其二)

杜 甫

浮云终日行，
游子久不至。
三夜频梦君，
情亲见君意。
告归常局促，
苦道来不易。
江湖多风波，
舟楫恐失坠。
出门搔白首，
若负平生志。
冠盖满京华，
斯人独憔悴。
孰云网恢恢，
将老身反累。
千秋万岁名，
寂寞身后事。

Looking Out on Spring

Du Fu

Our country has been completely crushed,
And only rivers and hills look the same;
The city is filled with tall trees
And the high grass of spring.
Even flowers seem to shed tears
For the sadness of our time,
The very birds
Grieve at the sight of people
Parting from their beloved.
Now for these three months
The beacon fires have flared
Unceasingly
While a letter from home
Is as precious as gold.
And, when I scratch my head,
I find my gray hair grown so sparse
The pin will no more hold it.

春 望

杜 甫

国破山河在，
城春草木深。
感时花溅泪，
恨别鸟惊心。
烽火连三月，
家书抵万金。
白头搔更短，
浑欲不胜簪。

Marching Beyond the Great Wall(I)

Du Fu

Sad it is to leave one's old home
For a long march to the North-west frontier!
Yet I must go: there are official times
For departures and arrivals,
And to desert would only lead to trouble.

We wonder why the Emperor,
Who has already so much good land,
Should want to send us to the frontier
To gain more;
Then, putting behind us love and warmth of parents,
And swallowing our tears,
We joined in the tumult of war.

前出塞(其一)

杜 甫

戚戚去故里，
悠悠赴交河①。
公家有程期，
亡命婴祸罗②。
君已富土境，
开边一何多！
弃绝父母恩，
吞声行负戈。

英汉对照
English-Chinese
中国文学宝库
Gems of Chinese Literature
古代文学系列
Classical Literature

① 交河：在新疆自治区吐鲁番县，是唐朝防吐蕃处。

② 婴：通撄，触犯。

Marching Beyond the Great Wall(Ⅵ)

Du Fu

In picking bows
Pick the strongest;
In choosing arrows
Choose the longest;
In killing men, first kill their horses;
In taking captives, first capture their commanders.

There should be a limit to the killing of men.
Every country should have its bounds.
It is enough to keep aggressors away;
No sense in killing and wounding so many.

前出塞(其六)

杜　甫

挽弓当挽强，
用箭当用长。
射人先射马，
擒贼先擒王。
杀人亦有限，
立国自有疆。
苟能制侵陵，
岂在多杀伤？

英汉对照
English-Chinese
中国文学宝库
Gems of Chinese Literature
古代文学系列
Classical Literature

Return to Qiang Village(I)

Du Fu

Towering clouds in the west grow crimson
As the setting sun comes down to the plain.
Sparrows twitter around the lattice gate,
And I, after all these miles, am home.

Wife and children, eyes wide with surprise,
Meet me, shedding many a quiet tear:
Not so easy, with all the world at war,
To have a man come home!

The neighbors' heads pop up over the garden wall;
Everywhere one hears sighs of surprise and welcome.
In the dead of night we sit by the light of a candle,
And I gaze into the faces of my dear ones, as if in a
dream.

羌村[①](其一)

杜 甫

峥嵘赤云西，
日脚下平地。
柴门鸟雀噪，
归客千里至。
妻孥怪我在，
惊定还拭泪。
世乱遭飘荡，
生还偶然遂。
邻人满墙头，
感叹亦歔欷。
夜阑更秉烛，
相对如梦寐。

① 羌村：至德二载八月(757年)，杜甫回鄜州的羌村探望家小。

英汉对照
English-Chinese
中国文学宝库
Gems of Chinese Literature
古代文学系列
Classical Literature

Return to Qiang Village(Ⅱ)

Du Fu

With my declining years consumed by war,
Even now home-coming yields me little joy.
My much-loved son staying close by my side,
Then, looking into my eyes, gets frightened, goes away.
I remember when I felt it was summer:
A time to explore cool places, walk under trees and around the pool.
Now I am back, and it is already winter, the north wind whistling,
And I am harassed by so many cares,
Yet comforted to know we have taken in
Our harvest, that the still has run,
And there is wine enough to give me heart
Through my declining days.

羌　村(其二)

杜　甫

晚岁迫偷生，
还家少欢趣。
娇儿不离膝，
畏我复却去。
忆昔好追凉，
故绕池边树。
萧萧北风劲，
抚事煎百虑。
赖知禾黍收，
已觉糟床注。
如今足斟酌，
且用慰迟暮。

Return to Qiang Village(Ⅲ)

Du Fu

Our cackling fowls were making such a din,
Fluttering and fighting when the guests arrived;
Only when I had chased them off up the trees
Did I hear the neighbors rapping at the gate.
There came a group of elders, four or five,
Each in his hand a present, greeting me
After my long journey. We sat, and together
Drank the wine that they had brought me
In wooden jugs.

"Poor stuff!" they said,
For the millet fields had not been ploughed,
The call for soldier's armor never ceased.
Sons had gone marching east with the army...
And I replied: "Let me sing a song for you,
My elders, of how sweet a thing it is to have
Your help in days of trouble..."
And after the song I sighed,
Gazed mutely at the heavens,
Then, looking into one another's eyes
We saw that all were wet with tears.

轮台歌奉送封大夫出师西征

岑 参

轮台城头夜吹角，
轮台城北旄头落①。
羽书昨夜过渠犁②，
单于已在金山西③。
戍楼西望烟尘黑，
汉兵屯在轮台北。
上将拥旄西出征，
平明吹笛大军行。
四边伐鼓雪海涌④，

① 旄头落：在古人看来有敌军必败之兆的意思。
② 渠犁：当时西域地区一军事重镇。
③ 单于：匈奴君主称号，这里借指敌酋。金山：阿尔泰山。
④ 雪海：天山一带的大片雪原。

Mount Yinshan[1] shakes amid our soldiers' roaring battle cry.
Heavily guarded enemy forts stretch to the cloudy horizon.
Bleached bones lay twined by tumbleweed on the battlefield.
By Sword River the wind is strong and snowflakes large,
At Sandy Gap the frozen rocks tear off the horses' hoofs.
Our vice-premier is ready to toil for the throne.
Pledging to pacify the borderland for the emperor's favour.
We all know the great events in the annals of history,
Now we'll see a heroic exploit overshadowing the past.

---

① In central Inner Mongolia Autonomous Region, also refers to the west frontier in general.

羌　村(其三)

杜　甫

群鸡正乱叫，
客至鸡斗争。
驱鸡上树木，
始闻叩柴荆。
父老四五人，
问我久远行。
手中各有携，
倾榼浊复清。
苦辞酒味薄，
黍地无人耕。
兵革既未息，
儿童尽东征。
请为父老歌，
艰难愧深情。
歌罢仰天叹，
四座泪纵横。

英汉对照
English-Chinese
中国文学宝库
Gems of Chinese Literature
古代文学系列
Classical Literature

Song of White Snow to Secretary Wu's Return to the Capital

Cen Shen

The north wind scrapes the ground, the fleabane broken,
In the borderland it starts snowing in the eighth month.
As though a gust of spring wind swept past overnight,
Bringing thousands upon thousands of pear trees into bloom.
It penetrates pearl blinds and moistens silk curtains,
The fox fur is cold, the brocade quilt too thin for the nip.
The general fails to draw his horn-backed bow steadily,
The viceroy can hardly put on his frigid iron mail.
A vast expanse of desert is covered with ice of a thousand feet,
Gloomy clouds hang over ten thousand miles of frozen land.
In the central camp a homebound colleague is wined and dined,
The music is played with fiddles, lutes and piccolos.

白雪歌送武判官归京

岑 参

北风卷地白草折，
胡天八月即飞雪。
忽如一夜春风来，
千树万树梨花开①。
散入珠帘湿罗幕②，
狐裘不暖锦衾薄③。
将军角弓不得控④，
都护铁衣冷犹著⑤。
瀚海阑干百丈冰⑥，
愁云惨淡万里凝。
中军置酒饮归客，
胡琴琵琶与羌笛⑦。

---

① 梨花：春天开放，花作白色，这里比喻雪花积在树枝上，像梨花开了一样。

② 珠帘：以珠子穿缀成的挂帘。罗幕：丝织帐幕。这句说雪花飞进珠帘，沾湿罗幕。

③ 锦衾(jīn)薄：盖了华美的织锦被子还觉得薄。形容天气很冷。

④ 角弓：饰有兽角的弓。控：拉开。这句说因为太冷，将军都拉不开弓了。

⑤ 著：穿上。

⑥ 瀚海：大沙漠。这句说大沙漠里到处都结着很厚的冰。

⑦ 胡琴等都是当时西域地区兄弟民族的乐器。这句说在饮酒时奏起了乐曲。

Evening snow keeps pouring down at the camp gate,
Wind tugs at the red standard but it's too frozen to flutter.
At the eastern city gate of Luntai[1] I shall see you off,
The road ahead along Tianshan Mountains[2] is heavy with snow.
As the path winds around the mountain and you are out of sight,
Tracks of your horse's hoofs will be left vainly in the snow.

---

① In present Miquan County, Xinjiang Uygur Autonomous Region.
② A big mountain chain ranging from east to west across the central part of Xinjiang Uygur Autonomous Region.

纷纷暮雪下辕门①，
风掣红旗冻不翻②。
轮台东门送君去③，
去时雪满天山路。
山迴路转不见君，
雪上空留马行处。

英汉对照
English-Chinese
中国文学宝库
Gems of Chinese Literature
古代文学系列
Classical Literature

① 辕门：军营的大门，临时用车辕架成，故称。
② 冻不翻：旗被风往一个方向吹，给人以冻住之感。
③ 轮台：唐轮台在今新疆维吾尔自治区米泉县，与汉轮台不是同一地方。

Song of Luntai to Chancellor Feng[1] on the Westbound Expedition

Cen Shen

On the city wall of Luntai horn-bugles sound at night,
North of Luntai town Pleiades is on the wane.
An urgent dispatch was sent past Quli[2] last night,
Tartar chief had arrived in the west of Gold Mountains[3].
Looking westward from the watchtowers dark smoke's rolling.
The government troops are stationed in the north of Luntai.
A great general holding the truncheon goes westward to war.
Playing flutes the mighty army marches off at dawn.
Snow Sea[4] surges amid our drum rataplan from all sides,

① Feng Changqing (?), a meritorious general and border region governor. The poet was a secretary under his command at the time.
② In present Luntai County, Xinjiang.
③ Altai Mountains in northwestern Xinjiang.
④ Between the highest peak of Tianshan Mountains and Issyk Lake, here it refers to the western region in general.

轮台歌奉送封大夫出师西征

岑 参

轮台城头夜吹角，
轮台城北旄头落①。
羽书昨夜过渠犁②，
单于已在金山西③。
戍楼西望烟尘黑，
汉兵屯在轮台北。
上将拥旄西出征，
平明吹笛大军行。
四边伐鼓雪海涌④，

① 旄头落：在古人看来有敌军必败之兆的意思。

② 渠犁：当时西域地区一军事重镇。

③ 单于：匈奴君主称号，这里借指敌首。金山：阿尔泰山。

④ 雪海：天山一带的大片雪原。

英汉对照
English-Chinese
中国文学宝库
Gems of Chinese Literature
古代文学系列
Classical Literature

Mount Yinshan[①] shakes amid our soldiers' roaring battle cry.
Heavily guarded enemy forts stretch to the cloudy horizon.
Bleached bones lay twined by tumbleweed on the battlefield.
By Sword River the wind is strong and snowflakes large,
At Sandy Gap the frozen rocks tear off the horses' hoofs.
Our vice-premier is ready to toil for the throne.
Pledging to pacify the borderland for the emperor's favour.
We all know the great events in the annals of history,
Now we'll see a heroic exploit overshadowing the past.

---

① In central Inner Mongolia Autonomous Region, also refers to the west frontier in general.

三军大呼阴山动①。
虏塞兵气连云屯②，
战场白骨缠草根。
剑河风急云片阔③，
沙口石冻马蹄脱④。
亚相勤王甘苦辛⑤，
誓将报主静边尘⑥。
古来青史谁不见？
今见功名胜古人。

---

① 阴山：非今内蒙阴山，天山古代可称阴山。
② 虏塞：敌方要塞。
③ 剑河：西域一河名。
④ 沙口：西域一地名。
⑤ 亚相：指封常清。御史大夫位在上卿，次于丞相，故称。勤王：操劳王事，为皇帝服务。
⑥ 静边尘：安定边疆。

Song of Walking-horse River to the Departure of the Army on the Westbound Expedition

Cen Shen

Have you not seen, along the Walking-horse River, [1]
Around the brink of Snow Sea,
The boundless swell of yellow sand soars up to the sky?
At Luntai the wind in the ninth month roars at night,
The riverbed is strewn with broken rocks big as bushel measures,
Which are lurching and rolling about with the sweeping wind.
In Tartar tribes grasses are yellow, horses stout and strong,
West of Gold Mountains smoke and dust are seen billowing,
A great general of the empire leads the army westward.
The general wears his golden armour all the night,
On the midnight march halberds brush and crash each other,
The piercing wind cutting the cheeks like a knife.

---

① In northwestern Xinjiang.

走马川行奉送封大夫出师西征

岑 参

君不见走马川行雪海边①，
平沙莽莽黄入天！
轮台九月风夜吼，
一川碎石大如斗，
随风满地石乱走。
匈奴草黄马正肥，
金山西见烟尘飞，
汉家大将② 西出师。
将军金甲夜不脱，
半夜军行戈相拨③，
风头如刀面如割。

① 走马川：一河谷名，在轮台之西。
② 汉家大将：指封常清。
③ 戈相拨：因夜色朦胧，行军时较长的兵器互相碰撞。

With snowflakes on their coats, the sweat evaporating,
The fine steeds and piebalds are soon clad in ice;
Ink freezes as the denunciation is drafted in the tent.
Enemy cavalry'd surely become terror-striken at the news,
They won't dare to engage us with swords at close quarters,
At Jushi's[1] western gate I'll await the triumphant display of booty.

① Around present Turpan County, Xinjiang.

马毛带雪汗气蒸，
五花连钱旋作冰①，
幕中草檄砚水凝②。
虏骑闻之应胆慑，
料知短兵不敢接，
车师西门伫献捷③！

① 五花、连钱：都是马名，以毛色花纹得名。旋：不久。
② 草檄(xí 习)：起草文书。
③ 伫献捷：等候着献俘报捷。

英汉对照
English-Chinese
中国文学宝库
Gems of Chinese Literature
古代文学系列
Classical Literature

The Old Peasant

Zhang Ji

In the hills lives a poor old peasant
Farming a few small patches of hilly land;
Sparse his crops, many the taxes, and he goes hungry
While grain in the state granaries turns to dust;
At the year's end his home is bare but for plough and hoe,
He takes his son up the mountain to gather acorns;
But the West River merchant has hundreds of bushels of pearls
And the dog on his boat gorges every day on meat.

野老歌

张　籍

老农家贫在山住，
耕种山田三四亩。
苗疏税多不得食，
输入官仓化为土①。
岁暮锄犁傍空室，
呼儿登山收橡实②。
西江贾客珠百斛，
船中养犬长食肉③。

① 苗疏：指因土地瘠薄，禾苗长得稀疏。化为土：指粮食在官仓中积压腐烂，成了尘土。
② 岁暮：年底。傍：靠。橡实：橡树的果实。
③ 西江：长江上游的一段。贾(gǔ 古)客：商人。

英汉对照
English-Chinese
中国文学宝库
Gems of Chinese Literature
古代文学系列
Classical Literature

The Cowherd's Song

Zhang Ji

I lead my buffaloes far away
For thick grow the crops round our village;
In the meadow a hungry crow pecks at their backs
And won't let me play on the ridge.
My herd scatters through grassy meadows,
The white calf lowing sometimes towards the reeds,
And I blow on a leaf to a friend across the dike
Who cracks his long whip in reply.
Browse well, all you buffaloes, and keep out of mischief
Or officers will come and cut off your horns.

牧童词

张　籍

远牧牛，
遶村四面禾黍稠①。
陂中饥乌啄牛背，
令我不得戏陇头②。
入陂草多牛散行，
白犊时向芦中鸣③。
隔堤吹叶应同伴，
还鼓长鞭三四声。
牛牛食草莫相触，
官家截尔头上角。

① 禾黍：通指农作物。稠：又多又密意思。
② 陂(bēi)：泽边坡岸长有水草的地方。乌：鸟名。即乌鸦。多群栖近村的树林丛中。陇头：通指高的坡岭。
③ "入陂"二句：来到水边的坡岸，青草毵毵。牛群四散开去，欢快地啃嚼起来，幼小的牛犊还不时对着芦苇丛"哞哞"地按；年年蠢子，虎患不休，可谓安宁无日了。

The Boatman's Song

Wang Jian

Pity me, born by a river port,
Conscripted onto two boats.
Hard days are many, good days few,
Like a seagull I sleep on the waves and trudge on sand.
Towed upstream against the wind the boat weighs a
hundred tons,
But the last stage and the next are poles apart;
At midnight we reach the dike in snow and sleet,
Out we're driven again as soon as we return.
Cold at night, wet through below our short coir capes,
Lungs bursting, feet bleeding — the pain is hard to bear.
Dawn breaks, but who will listen to our tale of woe?
Together we strain forward — yo-heave-ho!
A thatched hut may be worthless,
But what man can leave the home of his parents?
If I could change this water into land,
Then boatmen need no longer curse their fate.

水夫谣

王 建

苦哉生长当驿边，
官家使我牵驿船①。
辛苦日多乐日少，
水宿沙行如海鸟②。
逆风上水万斛重，
前驿迢迢波淼淼③。
半夜缘堤雪和雨，
受他驱遣还复去④。
寒夜衣湿披短蓑，
臆穿足裂忍痛何⑤？
到明辛苦无处说，
齐声腾踏牵船歌⑥。
一间茅屋何所值？
父母之乡去不得。
我愿此水作平田，
长使水夫不怨天。

① 驿：驿站。
② 水宿沙行：指纤夫夜宿船上，白日在沙洲上拉纤行走。
③ 斛（hú 胡）：量器名，古以十斗为斛，后又以五斗为斛。淼淼（miǎo 秒）：水势广远的样子。
④ 缘堤：指顺着堤走。他：指官家。
⑤ 臆穿：指纤绳在胸前磨擦，把胸口快磨破了。
⑥ 到明：到天亮时。腾踏：腾步踏地。

The Imperial Guard

Wang Jian

A notorious young man of Chang'an
Robbed a merchant downstairs and then got drunk upstairs,
Came off guard at dawn in the Palace of Brilliant Light
And fled to the pine forest on Mount Wuling;
He had murdered a hundred men and deserved to die,
But was pardoned for his "valour" in storming a town;
When news of this amnesty spread through the capital
He took his old name again in the register
And, coming out, rejoined the Imperial Guard,
Swaggering in front of the palace and shooting birds.

羽林行

王　建

长安恶少出名字，
楼下劫商楼上醉。
天明下直明光宫，
散入五陵松柏中。
百回杀人身合死，
赦书尚有收城功。
九衢一日消息定，
乡吏籍中重改姓。
出来依旧属羽林，
立在殿前射飞禽。

英汉对照
English-Chinese
中国文学宝库
Gems of Chinese Literature
古代文学系列
Classical Literature

Border Command Tower

Xue Tao

Looking out over clouds and birds, encircled by the autumn landscape,
Its majestic presence looms over forty southwestern prefectures.
I wish only that the generals will not covet the Qiang horses,
From the uppermost floor the boundary line is clearly visible.

筹边楼

薛　涛

平临云鸟八窗秋，
壮压西川十四州。
诸将莫贪羌族马，
最高层处见边头。

英汉对照
English-Chinese
中国文学宝库
Gems of Chinese Literature
古代文学系列
Classical Literature

Two Poems on the Lingyun Temple

Xue Tao

People talk of the Lingyun Temple moss,
Untouched by the sun's glare and fierce winds,
Like green cloud-shadows dropped on to crimson rock,
As though waiting for poets to come and sing of the moon.

People talk of the Lingyun Temple flowers,
Thrusting upwards around stone steps, leaning over the river;
Sometimes, trapped in the mirror of the moon goddess,
Like mythical multicoloured clouds.

赋凌云寺[①] (二首)

薛 涛

闻说凌云寺里苔，
风高日近绝纤埃。
横云点染芙蓉壁，
似待诗人宝月来[②]。

闻说凌云寺里花，
飞空透磴逐江斜。
有时锁得嫦娥镜，
镂出瑶台五色霞。

① 凌云寺：四川省乐山县东，有凌云山。唐、开元初，建凌云寺。开元中，僧海通凿山为弥勒大像高逾三百六十尺，建七层阁以复之，至韦皋镇蜀时，其工始备，皋作《大像记》。今呼其地为大佛岩。

② 宝月：北齐诗僧。

英汉对照
English-Chinese
中国文学宝库
Gems of Chinese Literature
古代文学系列
Classical Literature

To Wei After Being Exiled to the Borderland

Xue Tao

I heard that life in the border city was hard,
Only now do I begin to understand.
I would feel ashamed to sing those banquet songs
To people guarding the frontiers.

罚赴边上韦相公

薛　涛

闻道边域苦，
而今到始知。
羞将筵上曲，
唱与陇头儿。

英汉对照
English-Chinese
中国文学宝库
Gems of Chinese Literature
古代文学系列
Classical Literature

Recalling the Past at Mount Xisai

Liu Yuxi

Wang Jun's galleons sailed down from Yizhou, [1]
Jinling's[2] kingly grandeur faded sadly away:
Chain-barricades sank fathoms deep in the Yangtze,
Flags of surrender overspread the City of Stone[3].
Time and again men may lament the past;
The mountain remains unchanged, couched above cold river.
Now all within the Four Seas are one family,
By old ramparts autumn wind soughs through the reeds.

---

① Wang Jun (AD 206-285) led the troops of Jin down the Yangtzi River from Sichuan to conquer the Kingdom of Wu in AD 279.

② Jinling, present-day Nanjing in Jiangsu Province, was the capital of the Kingdom of Wu (AD 222-280) during the Three Kingdoms Period.

③ City of Stone was another name for present-day Nanjing.

西塞山怀古

刘禹锡

王濬楼船下益州，
金陵王气黯然收①。
千寻铁锁沉江底，
一片降幡出石头②。
人世几回伤往事，
山形依旧枕寒流③。
今逢四海为家日，
故垒萧萧芦荻秋④。

① 王濬(jùn 俊)：西晋武帝时益州刺史。楼船：大型战船。益州：州治在今四川省成都市。金陵：今江苏省南京市。

② 寻：古代八尺为一寻。铁锁：吴国知道晋将来攻，在长江险要处装置铁锁链以阻止晋水军，王濬用火炬烧毁了铁锁链，战船直抵石头城。降幡：表示投降的旗帜。

③ 往事：这里指东吴、东晋，及宋、齐、梁、陈破亡的历史。山形：指西塞山。枕：靠。寒流：指长江。

④ 四海为家：指国家统一。故垒：过去作战的营垒，这里指西塞山。萧萧：风声。芦荻秋：指秋风萧瑟，一片荒凉冷落景象。荻(dí 笛)，芦苇一类植物。

A Reply to Bai Juyi's Poem at Our Meeting in Yangzhou

Liu Yuxi

Cold and lonely the mountains of Ba, the rivers of Chu①,
Twenty-three years in exile,
Missing old friends, in vain I sang
The song of him who heard fluting②,
And home again I am like the woodcutter③
Who found his axe-handle rotted.
By the sunken barge a thousand sails go past,
Before the withered tree all is green in spring;
Hearing your song today, sir,
I drink a cup of wine and take fresh heart.

---

① The mountains of Ba and the rivers of Chu referred to far-off regions in southwest China.

② The singer who heard fluting was Xiang Xiu of the third century, who was reminded by flute music of his dead friends and wrote a poem about them. Here Liu Yuxi was thinking of Wang Shuwen and others of his associates who had died.

③ The woodcutter was Wang Zhi. According to a Jin-dynasty story, he went into the mountains to cut wood and stayed for a while with some immortals, returning home later only to find that his axe-handle had rotted away and all his neighbours were dead.

酬乐天扬州初逢席上见赠

刘禹锡

巴山楚水凄凉地，
二十三年弃置身①。
怀旧空吟闻笛赋，
到乡翻似烂柯人②。
沉舟侧畔千帆过，
病树前头万木春③。
今日听君歌一曲，
暂凭杯酒长精神④。

---

① 巴山楚水：泛指四川、湖广一带。二十三年：刘禹锡于唐顺宗永贞元年(805)九月被贬，到唐敬宗宝历二年(826)被召回，前后近二十三年。弃置：指被贬谪。

② 怀旧：怀念老朋友。闻笛赋：指晋向秀所作《思旧赋》。翻似：倒好像。烂柯人，据《述异记》载，晋代王质入山砍柴，遇见两个童子下棋，便停下来观看，棋还没有终局，见斧柄已烂，回到乡里，已过了百年，同时人都已死去。这里表现人世沧桑之感。

③ 侧畔：旁边。病树：指枯朽的树。万木春：指万木欣欣向荣，生机勃发。这两句比喻自己在政治上遭受打击，心中固然惆怅，却又相当达观，表现出豁达的情怀。

④ 君：指白居易。歌一曲：指白居易所作《醉后赠刘二十八使君》。

英汉对照
English-Chinese
中国文学宝库
Gems of Chinese Literature
古代文学系列
Classical Literature

A Willow Ballad

Liu Yuxi

North of the Pass, Qiang flutes played *Plum Blossom*[1];
South of the Huai, Xiao Shan sang *Fragrant Cassia*[2]
Play no more tunes, sir, of bygone dynasties
But listen to the new *Willow Ballads*.

---

① The Qiangs were a nomadic people in China's northwest. Plum Blossom was a local folk melody.

② Xiao Shan, a protégé of the Prince of Huainan (179-122 BC), wrote a poem in the traditional local style about fragrant cassia.

杨柳枝词(其一)

刘禹锡

塞北梅花羌笛吹，
淮南桂树小山词①。
请君莫奏前朝曲，
听唱新翻《杨柳枝》。

① 塞北：指我国北方边塞地区。梅花：指汉乐府民歌横吹曲的《梅花落》，到了唐代已经过时陈旧。羌笛：我国古代少数民族羌族的一种乐器。淮南小山：旧说为西汉时淮南王刘安的门客。桂树：指《楚辞·招隐士》，其第一句为"桂树丛生兮山之幽"。这两句是说，塞北用羌笛吹奏的《梅花落》，淮南小山的《招隐士》都已陈旧 。

The Old Charcoal Seller

Bai Juyi

The old man who sells charcoal
Cuts wood and fires his wares on the South Hill,
His face streaked with dust and ashes, grimed with smoke,
His temples grizzled, his ten fingers blackened.
The little money he makes is hardly enough
For clothing for his back, food for his belly;
But though his coat is thin he hopes for winter —
Cold weather will keep up the price of fuel.
At night a foot of snow falls outside the city,
At dawn his charcoal cart crushes ruts in the ice;
By the time the sun is high,
The ox is tired out and the old man hungry,
They rest in the slush outside the south gate of the market.
Then up canter two riders; who can they be?

卖炭翁

苦宫市也①

白居易

卖炭翁，
伐薪烧炭南山中②，
满面尘灰烟火色，
两鬓苍苍十指黑。
卖炭得钱何所营③？
身上衣裳口中食。
可怜身上衣正单，
心忧炭贱愿天寒。
夜来城外一尺雪，
晓驾炭车辗冰辙④。
牛困人饥日已高，
市南门外泥中歇。
翩翩两骑来是谁？

英汉对照
English-Chinese
中国文学宝库
Gems of Chinese Literature
古代文学系列
Classical Literature

① 作者自注。宫市：德宗贞元末年，宦官到市场上购买宫中所需的物品，看到其需要的东西，就口称“宫市”拿走，或象征性地给点钱，实际上是公开抢掠民间财物，所以市民看到他们就关门逃避。

② 伐薪：砍柴。南山：终南山，位于陕西省长安县南。

③ 营：谋。

④ 冰辙：冰雪冻结的车路。

Palace heralds in yellow jackets and white shirts;
They wave a decree, shout that these are imperial orders;
Then turn the cart, hoot at the ox and drag it north.
A whole cartload of charcoal, more than a thousand catties,
Yet they drive it off to the palace and he must accept
The strip of red gauze and the ten feet of silk
Which they fasten to the ox's horns as payment!

黄衣使者白衫儿①。
手把文书口称敕，
回车叱牛牵向北②。
一车炭，千余斤，
宫使驱将惜不得③。
半匹红纱一丈绫，
系向牛头充炭直④。

① 黄衣使者：宦官。唐代品级较高的宦官穿黄衣。白衫儿：指宦官中没有品级的随从。

② 把：拿。文书：公文。敕(chì 赤)：皇帝的命令。回车：拉转车子。叱牛：大声吆喝牛。牵向北：往北牵，唐皇宫在长安城的北部，东西两市在南边，所以要把牛往北牵。

③ 宫使：指宦官。驱：赶走。将：语助词。

④ 半匹：即二丈。绫：一种很薄的丝织品。充炭直：作为一车炭的代价。直，同“值”，价钱。

Song of Eternal Sorrow

Bai Juyi

Appreciating feminine charms,
The Han emperor sought a great beauty.
Throughout his empire he searched
For many years without success.
Then a daughter of the Yang family
Matured to womanhood.
Since she was secluded in her chamber,
None outside had seen her.
Yet with such beauty bestowed by fate,
How could she remain unknown?
One day she was chosen
To attend the emperor.
Glancing back and smiling,
She revealed a hundred charms.

长恨歌

白居易

汉皇重色思倾国①，
御宇多年求不得②。
杨家有女初长成③，
养在深闺人未识④。
天生丽质难自弃，
一朝选在君王侧。
回眸一笑百媚生，

---

① 汉皇：汉武帝刘彻，这里借指唐玄宗李隆基。倾国：美艳女子的代称，即绝代佳人的意思。

② 御宁：统治天下。

③ 杨家有女：指杨玉环，即杨贵妃。蒲州永乐（今山西永济县）人，开元二十三年（735）册封为玄宗之子寿王李瑁的妃子，后被玄宗看中，于开元二十八年（740）让她先出家度为女道士，住太真宫，赐名太真。至天宝四年（745）才正式将她纳入宫中，册封为贵妃。

④ "养在深闺"句：杨玉环早已做了寿王的妃子，这里所谓"养在深闺"，是诗人的曲笔，诗人不便把玄宗夺子妇的事说出来。

英汉对照
English-Chinese
中国文学宝库
Gems of Chinese Literature
古代文学系列
Classical Literature

All the powdered ladies of the six palaces
At once seemed dull and colourless.
One cold spring day she was ordered
To bathe in the Huaqing Palace baths.
The warm water slipped down
Her glistening jade-like body.
When her maids helped her rise,
She looked so frail and lovely,
At once she won the emperor's favour.
Her hair like a cloud,
Her face like a flower,
A gold hairpin adorning her tresses.
Behind the warm lotus-flower curtain,
They took their pleasure in the spring night.
Regretting only the spring nights were too short;
Rising only when the sun was high;
He stopped attending court sessions
In the early morning.
Constantly she amused and feasted with him,
Accompanying him on his spring outings,
Spending all the nights with him.
Though many beauties were in the palace,
More than three thousand of them,
All his favours were centred on her.

六宫粉黛无颜色①。
春寒赐浴华清池②,
温泉水滑洗凝脂③。
侍儿扶起娇无力,
始是新承恩泽时④。
云鬓花颜金步摇⑤,
芙蓉帐暖度春宵⑥。
春宵苦短日高起⑦,
从此君王不早朝⑧。
承欢侍宴无闲暇,
春从春游夜专夜。
后宫佳丽三千人,
三千宠爱在一身。

① 六宫:泛指后妃的住处。粉黛:原是妇女的化妆品,粉是擦脸的,黛是画眉的,这里的粉黛是宫中妇女的代称。

② 华清池:在今陕西省临潼县东南骊山上。

③ 凝脂:指杨贵妃肌肤洁白细嫩,如同凝聚的脂肪。

④ 始是:才是。新承恩泽:开始得到玄宗的宠爱。

⑤ 金步摇:妇女用的首饰,上有垂珠,行步时就摇动。

⑥ 芙蓉帐:带有荷花图案的帐子。

⑦ 苦短:苦于春夜的时间太短。日高起:太阳升得老高才起来。

⑧ 不早朝:是说玄宗贪恋女色,不上早朝,不理政事。

Finishing her coiffure in the gilded chamber,
Charming, she accompanied him at night.
Feasting together in the marble pavilion,
Inebriated in the spring.
All her sisters and brothers
Became nobles with fiefs.
How wonderful to have so much splendour
Centred in one family!
All parents wished for daughters
Instead of sons!
The Li Mountain lofty pleasure palace
Reached to the blue sky.
The sounds of heavenly music were carried
By the wind far and wide.
Gentle melodies and graceful dances
Mingled with the strings and flutes;
The emperor never tired of these.
Then battle drums shook the earth,
The alarm sounding from Yuyang.
The *Rainbow and Feather Garments Dance*
Was stopped by sounds of war.
Dust filled the high-towered capital,
As thousands of carriages and horsemen
Fled to the southwest.

金屋妆成娇侍夜，
玉楼宴罢醉和春①。
姊妹弟兄皆列土②，
可怜光彩生门户③。
遂令天下父母心④，
不重生男重生女。
骊宫高处入青云⑤，
仙乐风飘处处闻⑥。
缓歌慢舞凝丝竹⑦，
尽日君王看不足。
渔阳鼙鼓动地来⑧，
惊破霓裳羽衣曲⑨。
九重城阙烟尘生⑩，
千乘万骑西南行⑪。

---

① 玉楼：华美的楼台。醉和春：即醉意和着春意。

② 列土：分封领地。列，同裂。

③ 可怜：可爱，这里作可羡解。

④ 遂令：就使得。

⑤ 骊宫：指骊山的华清宫。

⑥ 仙乐：指华清宫的美妙音乐声。

⑦ “缓歌”句：是说轻慢的歌舞节拍与伴奏的音乐旋律极为吻合，凝合成了一个和谐的整体。丝，指弦乐器；竹，指管乐器。

⑧ 渔阳：唐代郡名，今北京市平谷一带。鼙(pi 皮)鼓：古代军中用的鼓，这里用以指战争。

⑨ 霓裳羽衣曲：唐代名曲，传为开元中西凉府节度使杨敬述所献的西域乐舞，初名《婆罗门曲》，后经唐玄宗润色，改名为《霓裳羽衣曲》。

⑩ 九重：指皇帝居住的地方。古代制度，皇宫由内到外有九道门，故称九重。城阙：指京城长安。烟尘生：指发生了战乱。

⑪ 西南行：向西南方前进，准备到四川去。

英汉对照
English-Chinese
中国文学宝库
Gems of Chinese Literature
古代文学系列
Classical Literature

The emperor's green-canopied carriage
Was forced to halt,
Having left the west city gate
More than a hundred *li*.
There was nothing the emperor could do,
At the army's refusal to proceed.
So she with the moth-like eyebrows
Was killed before his horses.
Her floral-patterned gilded box
Fell to the ground, abandoned and unwanted,
Like her jade hairpin
With the gold sparrow and green feathers.
Covering his face with his hands,
He could not save her.
Turning back to look at her,
His tears mingled with her blood.
Yellow dust filled the sky;
The wind was cold and shrill.
Ascending high winding mountain paths,
They reached the Sword Pass,

翠华摇摇行复止①，
西出都门百余里。
六军不发无奈何②，
宛转蛾眉马前死③。
花钿委地无人收④，
翠翘金雀玉搔头⑤。
君王掩面救不得，
回看血泪相和流⑥。
黄埃散漫风萧索⑦，
云栈萦纡登剑阁⑧。

---

① 翠华：指皇帝车驾上的旗帜，因是用翠鸟羽毛装饰的，故称翠华。行复止：指皇帝的车驾走走又停了下来。

② 六军：指给皇帝护驾的军队。不发：不肯前进。这句的意思是说，由于杨氏祸国，玄宗逃到马嵬驿时，护驾的将士不肯前进，龙武大将军陈玄礼发动兵变，杀了杨国忠等人，并逼着玄宗赐死杨妃。玄宗无可奈何，只得命高力士把杨妃缢死在佛堂。

③ 宛转：指杨妃临死时呻吟悱恻的样子。蛾眉：指美丽的女子，这里指杨妃。

④ 花钿(diàn 店)：镶嵌花纹的首饰。委地：丢落在地上。

⑤ 翠翘：妇女的首饰。金雀：金钗名。玉搔头：玉制的簪子。

⑥ 回看句：是写玄宗的伤痛，以至于血泪相和流。

⑦ 黄埃散漫：尘埃飞散。

⑧ 云栈：指高入云天的栈道。这是古代在险峻的山岩上用木头架设的通道，又称阁道。萦(yíng 营)纡(yū 迂)：回环曲折。剑阁：剑门山，在今四川省剑阁县北。

At the foot of the Emei Mountains.
Few came that way.
Their banners seemed less resplendent;
Even the sun seemed dim.
Though the rivers were deep blue,
And the Sichuan mountains green,
Night and day the emperor mourned.
In his refuge when he saw the moon,
Even it seemed sad and wan.
On rainy nights, the sound of bells
Seemed broken-hearted.
Fortunes changed, the emperor was restored.
His dragon-carriage started back.
Reaching the place where she died,
He lingered, reluctant to leave.
In the earth and dust of Mawei Slope,
No lady with the jade-like face was found.
The spot was desolate.
Emperor and servants exchanged looks,
Their clothes stained with tears.
Turning eastwards towards the capital,
They led their horses slowly back.
The palace was unchanged on his return,
With lotus blooming in the Taiye Pool
And willows in the Weiyang Palace.

峨嵋山下少人行，
旌旗无光日色薄①。
蜀江水碧蜀山青②，
圣主朝朝暮暮情③。
行宫见月伤心色，
夜雨闻铃肠断声④。
天旋地转回龙驭⑤，
到此踌躇不能去⑥。
马嵬坡下泥土中⑦，
不见玉颜空死处。
君臣相顾尽沾衣，
东望都门信马归。
归来池苑皆依旧⑧，
太液芙蓉未央柳⑨。

---

① 旌旗：旗帜。日色薄：形容日光黯淡。
② 蜀：蜀地，今四川省曾是古代蜀国的地方。
③ 圣主：指唐玄宗。
④ 铃：指行宫屋檐角上挂的铃铛。
⑤ 天旋地转：喻指时局发生重大变化。龙驭：(yù 玉)：皇帝的车驾。
⑥ 到此：指皇帝的车驾还京，来到了马嵬驿。不能去：不忍离去。
⑦ 马嵬坡：今陕西省兴平县西，即埋葬杨妃的地方。
⑧ 池苑(yuàn 院)：指宫中池子和园林。
⑨ 太液：太液池。汉代建章宫里的池名，在今陕西省西安市东。芙蓉：指水芙蓉，即荷花。未央：汉代宫名，故址在今西安市北。

The lotus flowers were like her face;
The willows like her eyebrows.
How could he refrain from tears
At their sight?
The spring wind returned at night;
The peach and plum trees blossomed again.
Plane leaves fell in the autumn rains.
Weeds choked the emperor's west palace;
Piles of red leaves on the unswept steps.
The hair of the young musicians of the Pear Garden
Turned to grey.
The green-clad maids of the spiced chambers
Were growing old.
At night when glow-worms flitted in the pavilion
He thought of her in silence.
The lonely lamp was nearly extinguished,
Yet still he could not sleep.
The slow sound of bells and drums
Was heard in the long night.
The Milky Way glimmered bright.
It was almost dawn.
Cold and frosty the paired-love-bird tiles;
Chilly the kingfisher-feathered quilt
With none to share it.

芙蓉如面柳如眉①，
对此如何不泪垂②。
春风桃李花开日，
秋雨梧桐叶落时。
西宫南内多秋草③，
落叶满阶红不扫④。
梨园弟子白发新⑤，
椒房阿监青娥老⑥。
夕殿萤飞思悄然⑦，
孤灯挑尽未成眠⑧。
迟迟钟鼓初长夜⑨，
耿耿星河欲曙天⑩。
鸳鸯瓦冷霜华重⑪，
翡翠衾寒谁与共⑫。

---

① “芙蓉如面”句是说，看到池中艳丽的荷花，就像看到了杨妃的脸；看到了那秀美的柳叶，就像看到她的眉毛。

② 对此：即对着“芙蓉如面柳如眉”的情景。

③ 西宫：即西内，指太极宫。南内：即兴庆宫，在宫城的南面，故称南内。

④ 红不扫：指秋天红叶落满庭阶也没人来扫去。

⑤ 梨园弟子：指玄宗当年在梨园训练的乐工。白发新：新添了白发。

⑥ 椒房：用花椒粉和泥涂壁，取其芳香，为后妃所住的宫室。阿监：宫中的女官。青娥：指宫女。

⑦ 夕殿：夜晚的宫殿。思悄然：意绪萧索，寂然无声。

⑧ “孤灯”句：一个人不断地挑着孤灯，把灯芯都烧尽了，人还睡不着。

⑨ 钟鼓：宫中报时辰的。初长夜：秋夜更长了。

⑩ 耿耿：明亮。

⑪ 鸳鸯瓦：两片一俯一仰，嵌合成对的瓦。

⑫ 翡翠衾：上面绣有翡翠鸟的被子。

Though she had died years before,
Her spirit never appeared even in his dreams.
A priest from Linqiong came to Chang'an,
Said to summon spirits at his will.
Moved by the emperor's longing for her,
He sent a magician to make a careful search.
Swift as lightning, through the air he sped,
Up to the heavens, below the earth, everywhere.
Though they searched the sky and nether regions,
Of her there was no sign.
Till he heard of a fairy mountain
In the ocean of a never-never land.
Ornated pavilions rose through coloured clouds,
Wherein dwelt lovely fairy folk.
One was named Taizhen,
With snowy skin and flowery beauty,
Suggesting that this might be she.

悠悠生死别经年①，
魂魄不曾来入梦。
临邛道士鸿都客②，
能以精诚致魂魄③。
为感君王展转思④，
遂教方士殷勤觅⑤。
排空驭气奔如电⑥，
升天入地求之遍⑦。
上穷碧落下黄泉⑧，
两处茫茫皆不见⑨。
忽闻海上有仙山⑩，
山在虚无缥缈间。
楼阁玲珑五云起⑪，
其中绰约多仙子⑫。
中有一人字太真⑬，
雪肤花貌参差是⑭。

---

① 悠悠：长远。经年：经过一年。

② 临邛(qióng 穷)：今四川省邛崃县。鸿都客：这是对从蜀地来的道士的美称。鸿都：东汉京城洛阳宫门名，是当时政府藏书的地方。

③ 精诚：真诚。这里是指道士的法术。致：招致，使来。

④ 展转思：翻来覆去的想念。

⑤ 殷勤觅：用心用意地寻找。

⑥ 排空驭气：腾云驾雾。

⑦ 之：指代杨妃。求之遍：到处去寻找她。

⑧ 碧落：道家称天为碧落。

⑨ 两处：即“碧落”和“黄泉”两处。

⑩ 仙山：指蓬莱山。

⑪ 五云：五色的云彩。

⑫ 绰约：轻盈柔美的样子。

⑬ 中有：指众仙中有。字太真：即杨妃。

⑭ 参(cēn)差(cī)是：仿佛就是。

When he knocked at the jade door
Of the gilded palace's west chamber,
A fairy maid, Xiaoyu, answered,
Reporting to another, Shuangcheng.
On hearing of the messenger
From the Han emperor,
She was startled from her sleep
Behind the gorgeous curtain.
Dressing, she drew it back,
Rising hesitantly.
The pearl curtains and silver screens
Opened in succession.
Her cloudy tresses were awry,
Just summoned from her sleep.
Without arranging her flower headdress,
She entered the hall.
The wind blew her fairy skirt,
Lifting it, as if she still danced
The *Rainbow and Feather Garments Dance.*
But her pale face was sad,
Tears filled her eyes,
Like a blossoming pear tree in spring,
With raindrops on its petals.
Controlling her feelings and looking away,
She thanked the emperor.

金阙西厢叩玉扃①,
转教小玉报双成②。
闻道汉家天子使③,
九华帐里梦魂惊。
揽衣推枕起徘徊,
珠箔银屏迤逦开④。
云髻半偏新睡觉⑤,
花冠不整下堂来。
风吹仙袂飘飖举,
犹似霓裳羽衣舞⑥。
玉容寂寞泪阑干⑦,
梨花一枝春带雨⑧。
含情凝睇谢君王⑨:

① 金阙:黄金作的宫阙。阙,门楼。玉扃(jiōng 垧):玉作的门。

② 小玉:战国时吴王夫差的女儿名小玉,这在唐代已成为婢女的通称。双成:姓董,传说中西王母的侍女。这里的小玉、双成都是借指为杨妃成仙后的侍女。

③ 汉家天子:借汉指唐,即唐玄宗李隆基。使:差来的人。

④ 珠箔(bó 泊):珠帘。迤(yǐ 以)逦(lǐ 里):曲折连绵的样子。

⑤ 云髻半偏:因刚起床,尚未梳妆,头上发髻偏在一边。新睡觉:刚刚睡醒起来。

⑥ 犹似:还好像。连上两句是说,杨妃匆匆走下堂来,风吹起了衣袖,那飘飘欲飞的样子,还像当年演奏《霓裳羽衣曲》时那么轻盈柔美。

⑦ 玉容:美丽的容颜。阑干:纵横的样子。

⑧ "梨花"句:比喻杨妃流泪时的动人形象。

⑨ 凝睇(dì 帝):眼神注视。

Since their parting she had not heard
His voice nor seen his face.
While she had been his first lady,
Their love had been ruptured.
Many years had passed
On Penglai fairy isle.
Turning her head,
She gazed down on the mortal world.
Chang'an could not be seen,
Only mist and dust.
She presented old mementos
To express her deep feeling.
Asking the messenger to take
The jewel box and the golden pin.
"I'll keep one half of the pin and box;
Breaking the golden pin
And keeping the jewel lid.
As long as our love lasts
Like jewels and gold,
We may meet again
In heaven or on earth."
Before they parted
She again sent this message,
Containing a pledge
Only she and the emperor knew.
In the Palace of Eternal Youth
On the seventh of the seventh moon,

"一别音容两渺茫①。
昭阳殿里恩爱绝②，
蓬莱宫中日月长③。
回头下望人寰处，
不见长安见尘雾。
惟将旧物表深情④，
钿合金钗寄将去⑤。
钗留一股合一扇⑥，
钗擘黄金合分钿⑦。
但教心似金钿坚，
天上人间会相见。"
临别殷勤重寄词⑧，
词中有誓两心知⑨。
七月七日长生殿⑩，

---

① 两渺茫：指玄宗与杨妃之间因长期隔绝而互相都不知道彼此的情况。

② 昭阳殿：汉代宫殿名，这里借指为杨妃生前所住的宫殿。

③ 蓬莱宫：仙人住的地方，这里是指杨妃死后所住的仙境。日月长：是说此后在蓬莱宫中的日子将是永久的了。

④ 惟将：只把。旧物：指生前玄宗给她的纪念物品，即下句所说的钿合、金钗。

⑤ 钿合：用黄金珠宝镶成花纹的盒子。

⑥ "钗留"句：钗有两股，留下一股。钿合两扇，留下一扇。

⑦ 擘(bò 簸)：分开。

⑧ 重寄词：再三托使者寄语玄宗。

⑨ 两心知：指所说的誓词只有她和玄宗两人知道。

⑩ 长生殿：骊山华清宫里的殿堂。

Alone they had whispered
To each other at midnight:
"In heaven we shall be birds
Flying side by side.
On earth flowering sprigs
On the same branch!"
Heaven and earth may not last for ever,
But this sorrow was eternal.

夜半无人私语时[1]：
“在天愿作比翼鸟，
在地愿为连理枝。”
天长地久有时尽，
此恨绵绵无绝期。

英汉对照
English-Chinese
中国文学宝库
Gems of Chinese Literature
古代文学系列
Classical Literature

① 私语：两人私下说的话。

Song of the Lute Player

Bai Juyi

In the tenth year of the reign of Yuanhe, I was demoted to the assistant prefectship of Jiujiang. The next autumn, while seeing a friend off at Pengpu, I heard someone strumming a lute in a boat at night, playing with the touch of a musician from the capital. I found upon inquiry that the lutist was a courtesan from Chang'an who had learned from the musicians Mu and Cao but growing old and losing her looks, she had married a merchant. Then I ordered drinks and asked her to play a few tunes. After playing, in deep distress, she told me of the pleasures of her youth and said now that her beauty had faded she was drifting from place to place by rivers and lakes. In my two years as an official away from the capital I had been resinged enough, my mind at peace, but moved by her tale that night I began to take my demotion and exile to heart. So I wrote a long poem and presented it to her. It has 612 words and I call it the Song of the Lute Player.

琵琶行

白居易

元和十年(815),余左迁九江郡司马①。明年秋,送客湓浦口,闻舟中夜弹琵琶者,听其音,铮铮然有京都声②。问其人,本长安倡女,尝学琵琶于穆、曹二善才,年长色衰,委身为贾人妇③。遂命酒,使快弹数曲;曲罢悯然④。自叙少小时欢乐事,今飘泊憔悴,转徙于江湖间⑤。余出官二年,恬然自安,感斯人言,是夕始觉有迁谪意⑥。因为长句,歌以赠之,凡六百一十二言,命曰《琵琶行》。

① 元和:唐宪宗李纯的年号。左迁:降职。九江郡:是隋置的郡名,唐改为江州,州治在今江西省九江市。下文"浔阳城"、"江州"均指九江一地。司马:官名,州刺史下面管军事的副职。

② 湓(pén 盆)浦口:湓水流入长江的地方,在九江城西。

③ 善才:唐代对琵琶艺人或曲师的通称。

④ 命酒:吩咐摆酒。悯:忧愁。

⑤ 转徙:辗转迁徙。

⑥ 自安:自以为安适。迁谪意:被贬谪的不愉快的心情。

By the Xunyang River a guest is seen off one night;
Chill the autumn, red the maple leaves and in flower the reeds;
The host alights from his horse, the guest is aboard,
They raise their cups to drink but have no music.
Drunk without joy, in sadness they must part;
At the time of parting the river seems steeped in moonlight;
Suddenly out on the water a lute is heard;
The host forgets to turn back, the guest delays going.
Seeking the sound in the dark, we ask who is the player.
The lute is silent; hesitant the reply.
Rowing closer, we ask if we may meet the musician,
Call for more wine, trim the lamp and resume our feast;
Only after a thousand entreaties does she appear,
Her face half-hidden behind the lute in her arms.
She tunes up and plucks the strings a few times,
Touching our hearts before even the tune is played;
Each chord strikes a pensive note
As if voicing the disillusion of a lifetime;
Her head is bent, her fingers stray over the strings
Pouring out the infinite sorrows of her heart.
Lightly she pinches in the strings, slowly she strums and plucks them;
First *The Rainbow Garments*, then *The Six Minor Notes*.

浔阳江头夜送客，
枫叶荻花秋瑟瑟。
主人下马客在船，
举酒欲饮无管弦①。
醉不成欢惨将别，
别时茫茫江浸月。
忽闻水上琵琶声，
主人忘归客不发。
寻声暗问弹者谁？
琵琶声停欲语迟。
移船相近邀相见，
添酒回灯重开宴②。
千呼万唤始出来，
犹抱琵琶半遮面。
转轴拨弦三两声，
未成曲调先有情③。
弦弦掩抑声声思，
似诉平生不得志④。
低眉信手续续弹，
说尽心中无限事。
轻拢慢捻抹复挑，
初为《霓裳》后《六幺》⑤。

① 主人下马客在船：是说作者下马到客人所在的船中送别客人。
② 回灯：把灯拨得更亮。
③ 转轴：拧转琵琶上的弦轴，以调音定调。
④ 掩抑：指声调低沉。思(sì四)：悲。
⑤ 拢、捻、抹、挑：指弹琵琶的各种不同的指法。《霓裳》、《六幺》：均为曲调名。

The high notes wail like pelting rain,
The low notes whisper like soft confidences;
Wailing and whispering interweave
Like pearls large and small cascading on a plate of jade,
Like a warbling oriole gliding below the blossom,
Like a mountain brook purling down a bank,
Till the brook turns to ice, the strings seem about snap,
About to snap, and for one instant all is still
Only an undertone of quiet grief
Is more poignant in the silence than any sound;
Then a silver bottle is smashed, out gushes the water,
Armoured riders charge, their swords and lances clang!
When the tune ends, she draws her pick full across
And the four strings give a sound like the tearing of silk.
Right and left of the boat all is silence —
We see only the autumn moon, silver in midstream.
Pensively she puts the pick between the strings,

大弦嘈嘈如急雨，
小弦切切如私语①。
嘈嘈切切错杂弹，
大珠小珠落玉盘。
间关莺语花底滑，
幽咽泉流冰下难②。
冰泉冷涩弦凝绝，
凝绝不通声渐歇③。
别有幽愁暗恨生，
此时无声胜有声。
银瓶乍破水浆迸，
铁骑突出刀枪鸣④。
曲终收拨当心画，
四弦一声如裂帛⑤。
东船西舫悄无言，
唯见江心秋月白。
沉吟放拨插弦中，

① 大弦：粗弦即低音弦。嘈嘈：形容声音沉重舒长。小弦：细弦即高音弦。切切：形容声音急促细碎。

② 间关：鸟声。这句形容乐声像黄莺的叫声在花底流过。冰下难：这是形容乐声像流动的泉水，呜咽难鸣。

③ 冰泉冷涩：形容乐声象结冰的泉水那样清冷凝涩。弦凝绝：弦声凝滞停顿。

④ "银瓶"两句是说，乐声像银瓶忽然破裂，水浆迸射；又像铁骑突出，刀枪齐鸣。这是形容乐声在稍停之后，忽又高扬起来。

⑤ 拨：弹琵琶的拨片。画：同"划"。当心画：用拨子从琵琶中部划过四弦，一般表示曲终。

Straightens her clothes, rises and composes herself.
She is, she says, a girl from the capital
Whose family once lived at the foot of Toad Hill.
At thirteen she learned to play the lute
And ranked first among the musicians;
Her playing was admired by the old masters,
Her looks were the envy of other courtesans;
Youths from wealthy districts vied in their gifts to engage her,
A single song brought her countless rolls of red silk;
Men smashed jewelled and silver trinkets to mark the beat;
Silk skirts as red as blood were stained by spilt wine.
Pleasure and laughter from one year to the next.
While the autumn moon and spring breeze passed unheeded.
Then her brother joined the army, her aunt died,
The days and nights slipped by and her beauty faded,
No more carriages and horsemen thronged her gate,
And growing old she became a merchant's wife.

整顿衣裳起敛容①。
自言本是京城女，
家在虾蟆陵下住②。
十三学得琵琶成，
名属教坊第一部③。
曲罢曾教善才伏，
妆成每被秋娘妒④。
五陵年少争缠头，
一曲红绡不知数⑤。
钿头云篦击节碎，
血色罗裙翻酒污⑥。
今年欢笑复明年，
秋月春风等闲度⑦。
弟走从军阿姨死，
暮去朝来颜色故⑧。
门前冷落车马稀，
老大嫁作商人妇。

---

① 敛容：对客人矜持而有礼貌的样子。

② 虾蟆陵：即下马陵，在唐代长安城东南曲江附近。

③ 教坊：唐代官办的教习歌舞技艺的机构。

④ 秋娘：当时长安著名的乐伎。

⑤ 五陵：长安城外地名，该处有汉高帝长陵，惠帝安陵，景帝阳陵，武帝茂陵和昭帝平陵。五陵年少：泛指当时达官贵人家的子弟。缠头：赠给歌舞女子的贵重丝织品，叫做缠头。绡：生丝制成的纺织品。

⑥ 钿(diàn 店)头云篦：两头饰有花钿的发篦。击节：打拍子。翻酒污：是说被同少年们戏谑时打翻的杯酒弄脏。

⑦ 秋月春风：这里指青春岁月。等闲度：随便打发过去了。

⑧ 阿姨：教坊中管歌女的头目。颜色故：容颜衰减。

The merchant thought only of profit: to seek it he leaves her.
Two months ago he went to Fuliang to buy tea,
Leaving her alone in the boat at the mouth of the river;
All around the moonlight is bright, the river is cold,
And late at night, dreaming of her girlhood,
She cries in her sleep, staining her rouged cheeks with tears.
The music of her lute has made me sigh,
And now she tells this plaintive tale of sorrow;
We are both ill-starred, drifting on the face of the earth;
No matter if we were strangers before this encounter.
Last year I bade the imperial city farewell;
A demoted official, I lay ill in Xunyang;
Xunyang is a paltry place without any music,
For one year I heard no wind instruments, no strings.
Now I live on the low, damp flat by the River Pen,
Round my house yellow reeds and bitter bamboos grow rife;
From dawn till dusk I hear no other sounds
But the wailing of night-jars and the moaning of apes.
On a day of spring blossoms by the river or moonlit night in autumn
I often call for wine and drink alone;

商人重利轻别离，
前月浮梁买茶去①。
去来江口守空船，
绕船月明江水寒②。
夜深忽梦少年事，
梦啼妆泪红阑干③。
我闻琵琶已叹息，
又闻此语重唧唧④。
同是天涯沦落人，
相逢何必曾相识！
我从去年辞帝京，
谪居卧病浔阳城⑤。
浔阳地僻无音乐，
终岁不闻丝竹声。
住近湓江地低湿，
黄芦苦竹绕宅生。
其间旦暮闻何物？
杜鹃啼血猿哀鸣⑥。
春江花朝秋月夜，
往往取酒还独倾。

① 浮梁：唐县名，即今江西景德镇市。
② 去来：自商人去浮梁以来。
③ 妆泪：眼泪与脸上的脂粉相混。红：指脸上的胭脂色。阑干：泪流纵横的样子。
④ 重：更加。唧唧：叹息声。
⑤ 帝京：指长安。
⑥ 杜鹃啼血：相传杜鹃鸟悲啼时，嘴里会流出血来。

英汉对照
English-Chinese
中国文学宝库
Gems of Chinese Literature
古代文学系列
Classical Literature

Of course, there are rustic songs and village pipes,
But their shrill discordant notes grate on my ears;
Tonight listening to your lute playing
Was like hearing fairy music; it gladdened my ears.
Don't refuse, but sit down and play another tune,
And I'll write a *Song of the Lute Player* for you.
Touched by my words, she stands there for some time,
Then goes back to her seat and plays with quickened tempo
Music sadder far than the first melody,
And at the sound not a man of us has dry eyes.
The assistant prefect of Jiangzhou is so moved
That his blue coat is wet with tears.

岂无山歌与村笛，
呕哑嘲哳难为听①。
今夜闻君琵琶语，
如听仙乐耳暂明②。
莫辞更坐弹一曲，
为君翻作琵琶行③。
感我此言良久立，
却坐促弦弦转急④。
凄凄不似向前声，
满座重闻皆掩泣⑤。
座中泣下谁最多？
江州司马青衫湿⑥。

① 呕哑嘲哳(zhā 渣)：都是象声词，指嘈杂难听的声音。
② 琵琶语：琵琶乐声。
③ 更座：重新坐下。翻作：依曲调翻成歌词。
④ 却坐：回到原来的位置坐下。促弦：把弦调紧。
⑤ 向前：刚才。
⑥ 青衫：黑色的官服，唐代低级官员(八品、九品)穿的。

Walking by Qiantang Lake in Spring

Bai Juyi

North of Gushan Monastery, west of the Jia Pavilion,
Water brims level with the bank, the clouds hang low;
Here and there, the first orioles are disputing for sunny trees,
Young swallows, just down from the eaves, peck in the spring mud.
The riot of flowers begins to dazzle the eye,
The short grass barely covers the horses' hooves;
I love best the east of the lake, and could stroll forever
On that white-sand embankment shaded by green willows.

钱塘湖春行

白居易

孤山寺北贾亭西，
水面初平云脚低①。
几处早莺争暖树，
谁家新燕啄春泥②。
乱花渐欲迷人眼，
浅草才能没马蹄③。
最爱湖东行不足，
绿杨阴里白沙堤④。

---

① 孤山：在今杭州西湖中后湖与外湖之间，山上有孤山寺。贾亭：杭州刺吏贾全于钱塘湖建亭，名贾公亭。水面初平：指春天湖水上涨，水平齐岸。云脚：雨前或雨后接近地面的云气叫做“云脚”。

② 争暖树：争着飞向向阳的树。啄：衔。

③ 乱：繁、多的意思。

④ 行不足：游赏得还不够。白沙堤：又名十锦塘，即今杭州西湖白堤。

Lodging in a Village North of the Hill of the Purple Pavilion

Bai Juyi

In the morning I climbed the Peak of the purple pavilion,
In the evening I lodged in the village under the hill;
The village elder was pleased that I had come
And in my honour opened a jar of wine;
Yet before the cups reached our lips,
Rough soldiers burst through the gate;
In purple uniform, with sword and axe,
Ten or more, an unruly band.
They snatched the wine from our table,
They seized the food from our plates;
My host made way and stood behind them,
His hands in his sleeves as though himself a guest.
In the yard was a noble tree
Planted thirty springs before;
In vain my host tried to save it,
They took their axes and felled it at the root.
They claimed they were collecting timber for building
And belonged to the Armies of the Holy Plan.
Better not complain, my host,
For their commander now stands high in favour.

宿紫阁山北村[1]

白居易

晨游紫阁峰，
暮宿山下村。
村老见予喜，
为予开一樽。
举杯未及饮，
暴卒来入门：
紫衣挟刀斧，
草草十馀人；
夺我席上酒，
掣我盘中飧。
主人退后立，
敛手反如宾。
中庭有奇树，
种来三十春。
主人惜不得，
持斧断其根。
口称“采造家，
身属神策军。”
主人慎勿语，
中尉正承恩。

① 紫阁山：终南山的一个支峰。

Song and Dance

Bai Juyi

The year draws to its close in the land of Qin,[1]
A great snow fills the imperial capital;
And in the snow, leaving court,
Are noble lords in purple and vermilion.
The noble can enjoy the wind and snow,
The wealthy have no fear of cold and hunger;
All their care is to build great mansions,
All their task the pursuit of pleasure.
Horses and carriages throng the vermilion entrance,
Song and dance last on by red candle-light in the pavilion
In high delight the guests sit close together,
Heated with wine they throw off their thick furs.
The host is head of the Board of Punishments,
The guest of honour is the Lord High Justice.
At midday the music and drinking start
And midnight sees no end to the merriment.
What do they care that in Wenxiang Gaol
Prisoners are freezing to death?

---

① Present-day Shaanxi, where Chang'an the Tang capital was situated.

歌　舞

白居易

秦城岁云暮①，
大雪满皇州。
雪中退朝者，
朱紫尽公侯：
贵有风云兴，
富无饥寒忧；
所营唯第宅，
所务在追游②；
朱轮车马客，
红烛歌舞楼；
欢酣促密坐，
醉暖脱重裘；
秋官为主人③，
廷尉居上头；
日中为一乐，
夜半不能休。
——岂知阌乡狱④，
中有冻死囚！

---

① 秦城：指当时都城长安。
② 追游：追逐遨游，恣为荒嬉之事。
③ 秋官：指刑部的官员，专掌刑法。
④ 阌(wén)乡：县名，在今河南西部、潼关与灵宝之间。

英汉对照
English-Chinese
中国文学宝库
Gems of Chinese Literature
古代文学系列
Classical Literature

The Brocade of the South

Bai Juyi

What can compare with the brocade of the south?
No gauze or satin this,
But rather the waterfall on Mount Tiantai
That plunges forty-five feet in the bright moonlight;
It has the rarest patterns,
White smoke misting the ground and snowy clusters of flowers.
Who weaves such brocade? Who wears it?
Poor girls by the streams of Yue, ladies in the palace.
Last year the imperial eunuch passed on the emperor's order:
Designs from Heaven should be woven on earth.
Here are flights of wild geese beyond the clouds in autumn,
Dyed the colour of water south of the Yangtze in spring.
The sleeves are wide, the skirt long;
Cut with golden scissors and smoothly pressed,
Its rare brightness is a foil for the strange designs,
And at every turn the flowers on it flash and quiver.
The dancer of Zhaoyang Palace is high in the emperor's favour,

缭 绫

白居易

缭绫缭绫何所似?
不似罗绡与纨绮;
应似天台山上明月前,
四十五尺瀑布泉。
中有文章又奇绝,
地铺白烟花簇雪。
织者何人衣者谁?
越溪寒女汉宫姬。
去年中使宣口敕,
天上取样人间织。
织为云外秋雁行,
染作江南春水色。
广裁衫袖长制裙,
金斗熨波刀剪纹。
异彩奇文相隐映,
转侧看花花不定。
昭阳舞人恩正深,

A set of her spring garments costs a thousand pieces of gold;
Once powder and sweat have stained them she discards them,
To be trailed through the dust and mud for all she cares.
To weave this brocade of the south is no easy task;
This is no ordinary satin or silk;
Holding many of these fine threads makes a girl's hand ache,
And the shuttle must clack a thousand times to weave less than one foot.
If the lady singing and dancing in Zhaoyang Palace
Could see the weaving, she would surely care for the brocade!

春衣一对直千金；
汗沾粉汙不再著，
曳土蹋泥无惜心。
缭绫织成费功绩，
莫比寻常缯与帛：
丝细缲多女手疼，
扎扎千声不盈尺。
昭阳殿里歌舞人，
若见织时应也惜！

英汉对照
English-Chinese
中国文学宝库
Gems of Chinese Literature
古代文学系列
Classical Literature

The Governor of Yanmen

Li He

Black clouds bear down upon the tottering town,
Armour glints like golden fish-scales in the sun,
Bugling invests the sky with autumn splendour
As crimson forts freeze in the purple dusk;
Red flags half-furled withdraw to the River Yi,
Our drums roll faint, muffled in heavy frost,
And to repay honour conferred from the golden dais①,
I draw my Jade Dragon Sword to die for my lord!

① The dais from which the governor received his appointment from the emperor.

雁门太守行

李　贺

黑云压城城欲摧，
甲光向日金鳞开①。
角色满天秋色里，
塞上燕脂凝夜紫②。
半卷红旗临易水，
霜重鼓寒声不起③。
报君黄金台上意，
提携玉龙为君死④。

① 黑云压城：形容战争形势很紧张。甲光：指铠甲迎着太阳发出的闪光。金鳞：是说像金色的鱼鳞。

② 燕脂：同“胭脂”。这里形容边塞土地的颜色。

③ 半卷红旗：指行军途中风力大，因而卷起红旗，减少阻力。易水：源出河北省易县。声不起：指鼓声低沉。

④ 黄金台上意：指君王的深恩厚意。黄金台，战国时燕昭王所筑，故址在今河北省易县东南。据说台上放置千金，以招揽人才。提携：拿起。玉龙：指宝剑。

Song of the Bronze Statue

Li He

In the eighth month of the first year of the Qinglong era, during the reign of Emperor Ming of Wei, the court ordered a palace officer to ride west and bring back the gilded bronze figure of an immortal holding a disc to catch dew made during the reign of Emperor Wu of Han, in order to set it up in the front court. When the palace officer removed the disc and took the statue to his carriage, the bronze figure shed tears. So Li Changji, descended from a prince of the House of Tang, wrote this song.

Gone that emperor of Maoling,
Rider through the autumn wind,
Whose horse neighs at night
And has passed without trace by dawn.
The fragrance of autumn lingers still
On those cassia trees by painted galleries,
But on every palace hall the green moss grows.
As Wei's envoy sets out to drive a thousand *li*

金铜仙人辞汉歌

李　贺

魏明帝青龙元年八月，诏宫官牵车西取汉孝武捧露盘仙人，欲立置前殿①。宫官既拆盘，仙人临载，乃潸然泪下②。唐诸王孙李长吉遂作《金铜仙人辞汉歌》③。

茂陵刘郎秋风客，
夜闻马嘶晓无迹④。
画栏桂树悬秋香，
三十六宫土花碧⑤。
魏官牵车指千里，

① 青龙：是魏明帝曹睿(ruì 锐)的一个年号。青龙元年：据《魏略》应为魏明帝景初元年(237)。诏：诏令，皇帝的命令。西取：魏建都洛阳，西汉建都长安，在洛阳西，魏明帝派官到长安拆运铜人，所以说“西取”。汉孝武：即汉武帝刘彻。前殿：殿前。

② 临载：当起运时。潸(shān 山)然：涕泪下流的样子。

③ 唐诸王孙李长吉：李贺是唐宗室郑王的后代，故自称“唐诸王孙”。

④ 茂陵：汉武帝墓，在今陕西省兴平县。刘郎：指汉武帝。秋风客：汉武帝曾作《秋风辞》，以此称他。

⑤ 画栏：指汉武帝宫殿里彩绘的栏杆。秋香：指桂花。三十六宫：汉代长安离宫有三十六所。土花：苔藓。

英汉对照
English-Chinese
中国文学宝库
Gems of Chinese Literature
古代文学系列
Classical Literature

The keen wind at the East Gate stings the statue's eyes...
From the ruined palace he brings nothing forth
But the moon-shaped disc of Han.
True to his lord, he sheds leaden tears.
And withered orchids by the Xianyang Road
See the traveller on his way.
Ah, if Heaven had a feeling heart, it too must grow old!
He bears the disc off alone
By the light of a desolate moon,
The town far behind him, muted its lapping waves.

东关酸风射眸子①。
空将汉月出宫门，
忆君清泪如铅水②。
衰兰送客咸阳道，
天若有情天亦老③。
携盘独出月荒凉，
渭城已远波声小④。

① 指：直指，直往。东关：函谷关。酸风：凄凉的风。眸(móu 谋)子：眼中的瞳人。

② 将：共，与。君：指汉武帝。

③ 客：指金铜仙人。咸阳：秦代都城，旧址在今陕西省咸阳市东，这里借指长安。咸阳道：当时由长安至洛阳的通道。

④ 盘：指金铜仙人所携之承露盘。渭城：即秦咸阳，这里借指长安。

The Old Man Quarrying Jade

Li He

Quarrying, quarrying,
For green translucent jade
To make pendants for beautiful ladies,
The old man goes cold and hungry
And the dragon chafes in his pool,
For the once clear waters of the Lan are troubled. ①
On rainy nights on the hill he feeds on acorns,
His tears endless as the nightingale's anguished song;
The Lan is surfeited with human lives,
Haunted by ghosts of the drowned for long centuries.
Wind and rain shriek through the cypress trees on the slope,
Ropes stretch green and sinuous down to the bed of the pool;
He thinks of his little ones in the poor, cold hut,
When on the steps leading up to the ruined terrace
He sees the vine called Heart-break.

---

① The Lan was a stream at Lantian near Chang'an, in the bed of which good jade was found.

老夫采玉歌

李 贺

采玉采玉须水碧，
琢作步摇徒好色①。
老夫饥寒龙为愁，
蓝溪水气无清白②。
夜雨岗头食蓁子，
杜鹃口血老夫泪③。
蓝溪之水厌生人，
身死千年恨溪水④。
斜山柏风雨如啸，
泉脚挂绳青袅袅⑤。
村寒白屋念娇婴，
古台石磴悬肠草⑥。

---

① 步摇：古代贵族妇女的一种发饰。徒：空，徒然。好色：指步摇色彩艳美。这句意思是：水碧雕琢成的步摇，色彩徒然很艳美。

② 蓝溪：蓝田山中产玉石的地方，在今陕西省蓝田县东南。

③ 杜鹃：又名子规，啼声凄哀。传说它叫的时候，嘴中会流出血来。

④ 生人：活人，指采玉工。

⑤ 袅袅(niǎo 鸟)：摇曳不定的样子。

⑥ 白屋：茅草屋。磴(dèng 邓)：石级。悬肠草：又叫思子蔓，蔓生植物。这两句意思是：采玉老夫看到古台石磴旁的思子蔓，禁不住想起家中的娇儿。

英汉对照
English-Chinese
中国文学宝库
Gems of Chinese Literature
古代文学系列
Classical Literature

A Parting Poem

Du Mu

Intimacy too deep for words,
Silent gazes across a wine glass
Even the candle shares our grief at parting
And sheds slows tears until dawn

赠　别

杜　牧

多情却似总无情，
惟觉笄前笑不成①。
蜡烛有心还惜别，
替人垂泪到天明。②

英汉对照
English-Chinese
中国文学宝库
Gems of Chinese Literature
古代文学系列
Classical Literature

① “多情”二句：越是多情，越显得像无情。别筵上，凄然相对，挤不出一丝儿笑影。

② “蜡烛”二句：蜡烛有烛心——真如有心人一样，为我们难分难舍的离别，它不断流泪，直到天明。

The Golden-Valley Garden[1]

Du Mu

The luxury and glory have vanished with the fragrant dust,
But pitilessly flows the stream and the grass still turns green in spring.
When birds cry plaintively in the east wind at dusk,
The falling petals remind me of the girl who committed suicide from the tower. [2]

---

① The sumptuous private garden of Shi Chong, a high official of the Jin Dynasty(AD265-420).

② Alluding to the tragic suicide of Green Pearl, Shi Chong's favourite concubine.

金谷园

杜　牧

繁华事散逐香尘①，
流水无情草自春②。
日暮东风怨啼鸟③，
落花犹似堕楼人④！

① “繁华”句：繁华的往事，随着芳香的尘屑消散无踪。香尘：《拾遗记》：“石季伦（即石崇）屑沈水之香如尘末，布象床上，使所爱者践之，无迹者赐以真珠。”按：石崇原为大官，又使人航海致富，故生活极为奢靡。

② “流水”句：流水照样潺湲，春草依然碧绿，它们对人事的种种变迁，似乎毫无感触。水：指谷水。发源于铁门县，东南流经金谷园，注入幘水。

③ “日暮”句：傍晚，东风送来鸟儿的叫声，如怨如慕。

④ “落花”句：落花飘然下坠，就像当年殉情自尽的美人！堕楼人：指绿珠。《晋书·石崇传》载：绿珠是石崇爱妾，美而艳。权臣孙秀派人来要她，石崇不答应，说：“绿珠吾所爱，不可得也。”孙秀恼羞成怒，便矫诏逮捕石崇。石崇被捕时，对绿珠说：“我今为尔得罪。”绿珠哭着说：“当效死于君前！”便自投于楼下而死。后石崇亦全家被杀。

Thoughts About My Past

Du Mu

In the South my life was dissolute — soaked in wine;
Wasp-waisted girls danced around me constantly.
Those days, ten years ago in Yangzhou, now seem like a dream,
With nothing gained but the reputation of being a dandy.

遣 怀

杜 牧

落拓江南载酒行①，
楚腰纤细掌中轻②。
十年一觉扬州梦，
赢得青楼薄倖名③。

① "落拓"句：我曾在江南放浪不羁地饮酒畅游。落拓(tuò 唾)：自由放纵，无拘无束。一作"落魄"。江南：一作江湖。这句写在淮南节度使幕府任职时的旧事。

② "楚腰"句：我爱那掌上起舞的纤细的腰肢。楚腰：美人的细腰。《韩非子·二柄》："楚灵王好细腰，而国中多饿人。"纤细：一作肠断。掌中轻：汉成帝的皇后赵飞燕体态轻盈，能在掌上起舞。

③ "十年"二句：一转眼，十年过去了，扬州的往事，恍如一梦。只在秦楼楚馆留下个"薄倖"的名声。赢得：一作占得。青楼：原指华美的楼房。曹植《美女篇》："青楼临大道，高门结重关。"杜牧此诗用以指歌楼妓院。后世遂以"青楼"专指妓院。薄倖(xìng 幸)：薄情负心。

英汉对照
English-Chinese
中国文学宝库
Gems of Chinese Literature
古代文学系列
Classical Literature

Climbing Mount Qi on the Ninth Day of the Ninth Lunar Month[1]

Du Mu

The waters reflect autumn scenes and wild geese start migrating.
Carrying wine flagons I ascend the green hill with friends.
There is seldom anything delightful in this mortal life,
I must wear chrysanthemums on my head on the way home.
It's best during this festival to drink up and get drunk,
No need to scale the heights and lament the setting of the sun.
Things have always proceeded like this,
Why should I cry about it like that duke did on Bull Hill?[2]

---

① Traditionally known as the Double Ninth Festival. It is the common practice in most part of China to climb up heights, drink wine and enjoy the chrysanthemum on that day.

② Alluding to Duke Jing of the State of Qi in the Spring and Autumn Period, who shed bitter tears when he viewed the splendid capital from the Bull Hill to the south of the city and was aware that he would die some day and part with the world.

九日齐山登高

杜　牧

江涵秋影雁初飞①，
与客携壶上翠微②。
尘世难逢开口笑，
菊花须插满头归③。
但将酩酊酬佳节，
不用登临怨落晖。
古往今来只如此，
牛山何必独沾衣！

---

① “江涵”句：秋色全映入澄彻的江水里，雁群开始南飞。涵：包容。

② “与客”句：正是携上酒肴，结伴登高的好天气。翠微：淡青的山色，指代山。《尔雅·释山》：“未及上，翠微。”疏云：“谓未及顶上，在旁陂陀之处。一说山气青缥色，故曰翠微也。”齐山有翠微亭，为当地名胜，俯瞰清溪，景色佳美，是杜牧在池州时所建。

③ “尘世”二句：人世间难得有开心的日子，今天要满头插上菊花，尽情乐它一乐！

In the Rainy Season of Spring

Du Mu

It drizzles endlessly during the rainy season in spring,
Travellers along the road look gloomy and miserable.
When I ask a shepherd boy where I can find a tavern,
He points at a distant hamlet nestling amidst apricot blossoms.

清 明

杜 牧

清明时节雨纷纷，
路上行人欲断魂①。
借问酒家何处有？
牧童遥指杏花村②。

① “清明”二句：清明时节，下着濛濛细雨，路上的行人，一个个神色黯然。断魂：伤心的样子。

② “借问”二句：“请问，哪儿有酒店？”牧童远远指着杏花深处的村庄。杏花村：由于杜牧此诗的影响，有好几处地方都起名“杏花村”。如著名的汾酒，便是山西汾阳杏花村酒厂出品。

Mooring on the Qinhuai River

Du Mu

The chilly water is shrouded in mist and the sand bathed in moonlight,
As I moor at night on the Qinhuai River near the taverns.
The singsong girls are ignorant of the tragedy of a lost regime,
They are still singing the *Backyard Flowers*[1] beyond the river!

① Alluding to *Jade Trees and Backyard Flowers*, a song composed by the last emperor of the Southern Dynasties, which was later considered a bad omen.

泊秦淮

杜　牧

烟笼寒水月笼沙①，
夜泊秦淮近酒家②。
商女不知亡国恨，
隔江犹唱《后庭花》③！

① “烟笼”句：薄雾笼罩着清凉的水面，月色映照着两岸的浅滩。

② “夜泊”句：晚上，我的船停靠在秦淮河，那喧闹的酒楼附近。当时金陵城内的秦淮河两岸酒家林立，是个纸醉金迷的花花世界。

③ “商女”二句：卖唱的姐儿不晓得亡国的愁恨，隔着江面，竟唱起了《玉树后庭花》。商女：卖唱的歌女。江：指秦淮河。后庭花：《玉树后庭花》的省称，是陈朝末代皇帝陈叔宝（陈后主）所作乐曲。陈后主耽于声色，不理政事，每天和妃嫔、狎客饮酒寻欢，终至亡国。所以人们把他作的靡靡之音《玉树后庭花》称为“亡国之音”。

英汉对照
English-Chinese
中国文学宝库
Gems of Chinese Literature
古代文学系列
Classical Literature

Travelling in the Mountains

Du Mu

A flag-stone path winds up into the chilly hills,
Where houses are just discernible amid the thick white cloud.
I stop my carriage for I love the maple trees in the twilight,
The leaves after early frost are as crimson as spring flowers.

山 行

杜 牧

远上寒山石径斜①，
白云生处有人家②。
停车坐爱枫林晚③，
霜叶红于二月花！

① 寒山：深秋时节的山。
② 白云生处：指山林的最深处，远望白云层生。
③ 坐：因。晚：夕阳晚照。

In the Autumn Night

Du Mu

Silvery candlelight flickers cheerlessly on painted screens,
As she whisks away the flitting fireflies with a small gauze fan.
The moonlight over the palace stone stairs looks like the cool water,
As she sits looking up at the Cowherd and the Woman Weaver. ①

① They are the legendary names of two bright stars. Altair and Vega, who are a pair of young lovers separated by the Milky Way and can only meet once a year.

秋　夕

杜　牧

银烛秋光冷画屏①，
轻罗小扇扑流萤②。
天阶夜色凉如水，
坐看牵牛织女星③。

① “银烛”句：乳白的蜡烛在秋夜发出寒光，冷冷地照着画屏。银烛：一作红烛。画屏：绘画的屏风。

② “轻罗”句：挥动轻巧的团扇，扑打着流萤。轻罗小扇：即纨扇、团扇，用轻薄的丝织品（罗）制成，圆形。

③ “天阶”二句：阶前的夜色水一样清凉，把牵牛、织女星细细仰望。天阶：皇宫里的石阶。天，一作瑶。阶，一作街。夜色：指夜间的光气。坐：一作卧。按：牛、女喻夫妇，末句不露形迹地表达了深闭内廷的宫女对自由的爱情生活的渴望。

The Gorgeous Zither

Li Shangyin

For no reason the gorgeous zither has fifty strings,
Each string, each fret, recalls a youthful year.
Master Zhuang woke from a dream puzzled by a butterfly, [1]
Emperor Wang reposed his amorous heart to the cuckoo. [2]
The moon shines on the sea, pearls look like tears,
The sun is warm at Lantian, [3] the jade emits mist.
This feeling might have become a memory to recall,
But, even then, it was already suggestive of sorrows.

---

① According to a fabled story, Zhuang Zi (c. 369-286 BC), a famous philosopher of the Warring States Period, dreamt of being a butterfly and when he woke up, he was so confused that he could not tell whether it was him that had dreamt of being a butterfly or it was a butterfly that was then dreaming of being him.

② A legendary king who had an affair with his prime minister's wife and after his death his spirit changed into the cuckoo.

③ A hill famous for its jade in present-day Lantian County, Shaanxi Province.

锦　瑟

李商隐

锦瑟无端五十弦，
一弦一柱思华年①。
庄生晓梦迷蝴蝶，
望帝春心托杜鹃②。
沧海月明珠有泪，
蓝田日暖玉生烟③。
此情可待成追忆，
只是当时已惘然。

---

① 锦瑟：彩绘如锦绣一般华美的瑟。瑟：一种弦乐器。无端：无缘无故地，不知为什么。柱：系弦的支柱，每弦一柱。

② 庄生：指庄周。晓梦：梦醒了。迷蝴蝶：为蝴蝶梦所迷惑。《庄子·齐物论》说：一次庄子梦见自己化为蝴蝶，觉得自己就是真蝴蝶了，便不知自己是庄子，不久梦醒过来，又觉得自己真是庄子，而不是蝴蝶。望帝：传说中的古蜀国的一个君主的称号，名杜宇，死后魂魄化为杜鹃鸟，啼声哀切。春心：伤春的情思。指望帝失国的悲痛。托杜鹃：是说望帝把他的悲痛寄托在杜鹃哀切的啼声中。

③ 珠有泪：《博物志》说，南海之外，有鲛人，他哭泣时流下的眼泪，就是亮晶晶的珠子。蓝田：即蓝田山，在今陕西省蓝田县，因山上产玉，又名玉山。玉生烟：指在阳光照耀下玉山所散发出的烟霭。这两句以“沧海月明”、“蓝田日暖”比喻自己所追求的美好理想，以“珠有泪”、“玉生烟”比喻理想的幻灭。意思是说，美好的理想，像鲛人的泪珠洒落海中，终成泡影；像玉山上升起的烟霭，随风飘散。

Cicada

Li Shangyin

Existing on your high place, your belly can hardly be full,
All in vain is your resentful shrill.
At dawn the intermittent cry is about to cease,
But the tree remains indifferently green.
A peach-wood idol adrift[1], to the court a petty servant,
My garden by weeds is overrun.
Much I'm obliged to you for your admonition,
I too, with my family, live in dire want.

① The allusion is taken from a fabled dialogue between a peach-wood idol and a clay idol, which reflects their respective helpless situation in the coming rainfall and flood.

蝉

李商隐

本以高难饱，
徒劳恨费声①。
五更疏欲断，
一树碧无情②。
薄宦梗犹泛，
故园芜已平③。
烦君最相警，
我亦举家清④。

---

① 以高难饱：古人认为蝉栖高树，是餐风饮露的，因此把蝉当作高洁的象征。这句是说，既栖高树，自然是难以饱腹的。这里的“高”字，意义双关，既指蝉的高栖，又指蝉的高洁。费声：枉费鸣声。

② 疏欲断：是说蝉长夜悲鸣，到天亮时，已力竭声嘶，稀疏到要断绝了。碧无情：是说蝉哀鸣树上，而树色依然如故，毫不动情。

③ 薄宦：卑微的官职。梗犹泛：喻指行踪飘泊无定。梗，树枝。泛：漂浮。芜已平：是说丛生的杂草，快要把故园平没了。

④ 烦：劳，麻烦。君：指蝉。最相警：最能使人警觉。举家清：全家清苦。

英汉对照
English-Chinese
中国文学宝库
Gems of Chinese Literature
古代文学系列
Classical Literature

Untitled

Li Shangyin

The stars of last night, the breeze of last night,
West of the Painted Bower, east of the Osmanthus Hall.
We can't fly wing to wing like a pair of phoenixes,
Yet our hearts closely linked beat in harmony.
Maybe you're gaming over a cup of warm spring wine,
Or perhaps betting with friends in the red candlelight.
Alas! The drumbeat at dawn calls me to my duties,
I must ride to the Royal Secretariat like a tumbleweed adrift.

无题二首(其一)

李商隐

昨夜星辰昨夜风，
画楼西畔桂堂东①。
身无彩凤双飞翼，
心有灵犀一点通②。
隔座送钩春酒暖，
分曹射覆蜡灯红③。
嗟余听鼓应官去，
走马兰台类转蓬④。

① 画楼：彩绘华丽的高楼。桂堂：形容厅堂芳美。

② 灵犀：指犀牛角。传说犀牛是灵异之兽，角上有条白纹，从角端直通大脑，感应灵敏，所以称灵犀。这里借喻彼此心意相通。

③ 送钩：将钩藏于手中叫人猜的游戏。分曹：分队。射覆：把东西覆盖在器皿下叫人猜，也是古代的一种游戏。

④ 鼓：报晓的更鼓。兰台：唐高宗龙朔初年，改称秘书省为兰台。类：似。

To Readers of the English Translations of Classical Chinese Prose and Poetry:

Chinese classical literature has a very long history. Some of the earliest works have left us questions that have baffled literary researchers for centuries. It has been difficult to find out the authors of some works, to interpret particular phrases and sentences, or to confirm the reliability of various versions of certain works. This gives rise to some questions in reading these translations. Here are some explanatory remarks.

Perhaps the earliest fables are taken from arguments of rhetoricians of the Spring and Autumn and Warring State periods, a tumultuous age when different schools of thoughts contended heatedly. Their debates and arguments were recorded in different books. Those rhetoricians were good at inventing witty parables, sometimes using animals as heroes, to support their opinions about certain events or people. Some fables were too closely bound with their contexts without which their morals might seem obscure (— if you find it hard to get the points of some fables, please remember this.) They were originally part of speeches and therefore had no definite titles. Some of the titles added later to them have been well accepted and even have become idioms in everyday Chinese, while others are just improvisations.

Similarly, the titles of some prose works were added by later editors or publishers. Some early books have been lost and today we can only see fragments of them in literary collections and anthologies. Often, different collections have different versions of the same pieces. That's why sometimes you see different titles for the same works or find details missing from or added to some stories.

The titles for the so-called *ci* poems are very peculiar. To understand them one must know the origin of that genre. "*Ci*" literally meaning "words" were words of songs. They were sung to music. Early *ci* were created by non-literati musicians active at the grassroots level. Their songs were much livelier and freer than scholars' creation, conveying ordinary people's aspirations and feelings. But since there are fewer musicians than poets, people tend to adapt the same melodies to new words. Just as we sing to the same tune the words: "In the canyon, in the... oh my darling Clementine..." and "Happy new year, happy new year, happy new year to you all..."; or, "Twinkle, twinkle little star..." and "A B C D E F G...". Later on literati writers took up this form of poetry. But since not many writers could compose music, they simply imitated the forms of existing songs and thus their works consisted of verses of different lengths. The "words" were finally divorced from the music (there have been, of course, exceptions — few *ci* poets, such as Jiang Kui, were good musicians and they created new forms). Unfortunately, in translation the forms of *ci* disappear. The reader of English translations usually cannot see much difference between the *ci* and other forms of classical Chinese poetry. Originally each song had a title reflecting its contents. When the same melody was adapted to new words, the title remained. By and by the title became irrelevant to the contents. Writers used the title as an indication of the pattern of forms used. Still later when the music was lost, *ci* simply became names of verse forms. Most *ci* writers entitled their works only by the names of the melodies and, occasionally, they give their works subtitles that reflect the contents. Different translators handle the titles in different ways. Some translators have tried to render the meaning of the titles in English. But since today the meanings of those titles are irrelevant to the contents of the *ci* poems, the semantic interpretation of the titles may sound queer and be meaningless. For the *ci* poems which have only the melody names as their titles some translators have given new titles indicative of the meaning of the whole piece (which may be helpful to English-speaking readers). To give a uniform appearance to our series, we rearranged the titles of *ci* poems, using the names of melodies as the titles which are merely transliterations from Chinese. We have kept the original subtitles added by the authors but cut the titles added by translators.

The translations of these classical Chinese works have been done through several decades and by different hands. They are in different styles and in terms of quality, they are not necessarily equally satisfactory. Sometimes the ambiguity lies in the structure of the Chinese language. For example, in Li Qingzhao's poem to the tune of *Yong Yu Le*, the following line "人在何处" (where is the person) has different interpretations: 人 may be understood as "I" or someone else. One translator rendered this line as: "where has my love gone." According to another interpretation, this line may be translated as "where am I now." Since absolutely "accurate" translation is not always possible and different translators naturally have different interpretations, by and large we have left the translations as they first appeared. We have done a few changes only where we thought the original rendering [illegible]ight have been too misleading.

[illegible] there are any errors caused by our editing, we beg the [illegible]on of our translators and readers.

Revisor

关于中国古典文学作品英译文的说明

这些作品的译文都是在《中国文学》杂志英文版上发表过的，不是完成于一时一人之手，译文风格各异，质量也不尽整齐。古书版本歧异，加之古代汉语与现代汉语差别很大，不同的人对某些字句也会有不同的理解（因此读者可能会发现某些译文与汉语原文注释不吻合）。此次分类结集出版，除极个别明显误译的字句外一般不作改动。中国古代寓言有很多取自先秦诸家言论集，大多是为论证某一论点而即兴编造的，有些寓言脱离原来的上下文后不易懂其要旨，某些寓言原文太简，有的译者在译文中加以适当的润饰，使现代读者读来更有趣味，凡是基本不背离原文原意[illegible]就保留了原译者的译文。有些古代散文作品原书已佚，今天只能散见[illegible]种文集中，不同文集所收同一作品字句常有出入，甚至题目也是后[illegible]的，因此读者可能会发现同一文章的不同题目和不同文字。考虑到本丛书是一般欣赏和学习读物，我们未作版本方面的考证。吕叔湘说得好，译诗无直译意译之分，唯有平实与工巧之别。本丛书所收的诗歌译文，有的紧扣原文，有的发挥较多。读者见仁见智，可以自己去比较。词历来多以词牌名为题，其字面义每与词意了不相干（如一首“西江月”可能根本不写“江”“月”）。不同译者常有不同的处理方法，如有的译者根据词的内容另拟新题，有的译者则把原词牌名意译。此次出版一律以音译词牌名作为词的题目，有原作者所加题目的保留原题作为副题。这样处理是否合适，请读者指点，并请原译者鉴谅。

——校译者